ꟷHE PROPHETS
.GES
BC

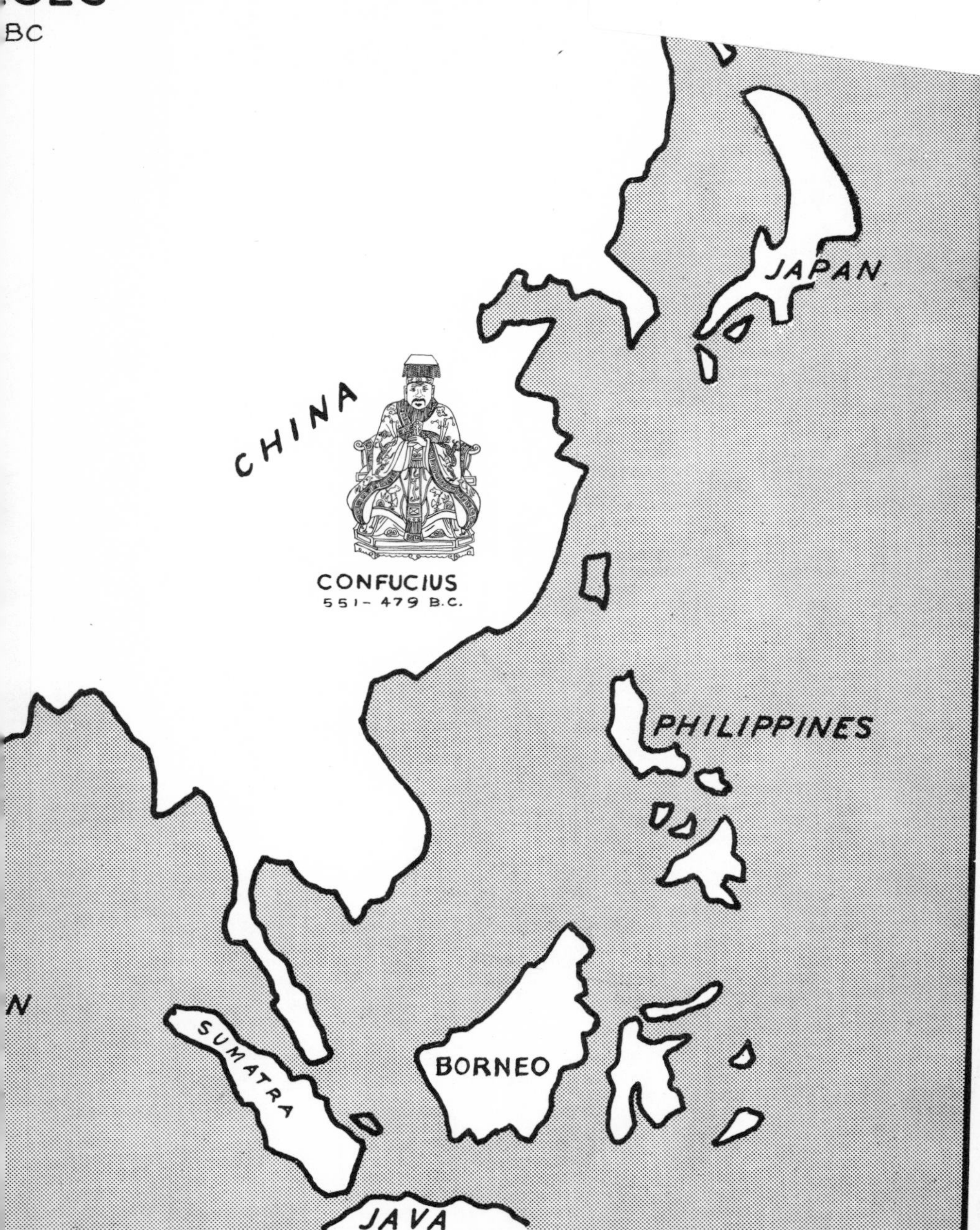

GOD'S HAND IN HISTORY

Book One: PIONEERS

BY

MARY WILSON

Illustrated by Vera Louise Drysdale

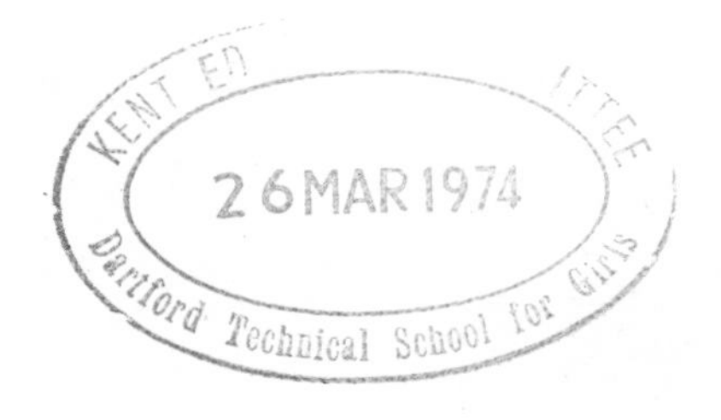

LONDON
BLANDFORD PRESS

First published 1960

167 *High Holborn, London, WC1V* 6PH

Second Edition, 1971

I am grateful to the many friends from all parts of the world whose wisdom and experience has contributed to the creation of this book, and especially to the late Dr. Frank Buchman but for whom I should not have found the faith that made the Bible come alive.

M.F.W.

Printed in Great Britain by
Jarrold and Sons Ltd, Norwich

Preface

WHEN our child was quite small she asked me to tell her a story. So I started writing from day to day the most gripping story I knew, that of God's plan for the world. I thought of it originally as a book in three parts about God the Father, God the Son and God the Holy Spirit, but naturally the period beginning with the Acts of the Apostles and lasting till the present day is longer than will fit into one volume. So I worked on; and there are now four volumes in the series.

The interest aroused in these books, in our own home, and later as a course of lessons in a small school, developed far beyond both. The series as it grew has been distributed all round the world, and has been used in the English language in schools and homes of every background and faith.

History today is recognised as more than a record of events. Karl Marx, for instance, says that it grows inevitably out of the clash of the materialistic forces of class, economics and environment. The battle between Good and Evil is, however, older and more ever-present, and has affected history from the earliest times.

As this first volume comes up for reprint, more than ten years after the launching of the series, the battle is intensifying, and is becoming more relevant than ever before in the societies of the modern world. Today a widening circle of children are coming to understand the fundamental struggle in the world, the battle that goes on in the heart of everyone between Good and Evil.

Unfortunately, it is becoming clear that among a growing number of people this battle is intentionally not being fought. The great conception of God as the Master Planner is being deliberately destroyed and the faith and moral sense of the rising generation is being systematically whittled away.

One index of this is an unparalleled crime rate among young people. Unless the landslide of immorality is halted, we are at the end of our present civilisation, and society as we have known it, including the Christian conception of the family, will come to an end. Many parents have already so jettisoned the moral code in their own lives that they can no longer tell their children the difference between right and wrong.

This book was written in the conviction that quite young children could be introduced to the real ideological struggle and take their place in it. They can learn that history is made by men and women who either moved courageously towards moral decisions, based on listening to the voice of God, or ran away from them. One approach is to study the early pioneers in this field and learn from them.

So we began with an account of the battle which has come down to us from the dawn of history and traced the story through a family and nation whom God specially chose to carry His Plan forward. The children followed the struggle with keen interest and identification through the growth and development of the Jewish people. Then before coming to the climax of the story, the earthly life of Christ Himself, we turned to look at some of the wise men of other races and places who in their own way were God's instruments, and played their part in the whole design.

The later books trace the expanding story of change which has come to the whole human family by means of men and women who obeyed God's Voice. Only a fraction of them can be told in books of this size and scope, but they all follow the same pattern of a call to obedience which affected nations. Of course they also show what happened when people did not obey.

Against this perspective living straight assumes a wholly new purpose. Boys and girls of any age who see no point in simply obeying rules and being good as an end in itself, eagerly respond to the thought of being in the historic succession of those who have fought to restore God to leadership in the world. In fact, as one child said towards the end of the book, 'Is this the part where we come in?'

Mary Wilson

CONTENTS

God's Plan for the World

IN the beginning God made the world.

At first the earth had no shape. A teacher explaining it to some children once said that it was runny, like treacle. You know how when you help yourself to treacle, you have to turn the spoon quickly to make the treacle wrap round it.

This is what God did with the earth. He set the hot runny mass twirling round the heavens, and as it turned it cooled and became steamy, and the steam became water. After a while some of the water dried off and the land began to appear. All the bits of land were of different shapes, and in time they became different countries. But to begin with there was nothing but the earth and the water, or land and sea.

God put the earth in the sky with the moon and the stars to shine by night and the sun to shine by day. He made trees and grass and flowers.

Then He made creatures to live in the world, fishes in the water, birds in the air and animals on the earth.

Next He needed people on the earth to love and look after. So He made man, and He made him in two parts, a body and a spirit. He gave him a body to live on the earth for a while, and help Him work out His Plan for the world. The spirit was to make the body live, and would come to be with God when man's time on earth was over.

But man was lonely, and God gave him a wife. So families began, father, mother and children.

Now God had a wonderful world with people and animals, birds and beasts, trees and flowers, and the sun, moon and stars shining on it.

He had angels to help Him. The angels wanted to work with Him to make the earth a happy place. But there was one who did not. He is called by different names, such as Satan or the Devil. He said he would not help God, nor help people to obey God; and God said, 'Then you must go away.' So he left the good angels, and became the Bad Voice who talks to us and tries to stop us doing what God says.

The first time we hear of this voice was in a beautiful garden which God had made for the first man and woman, who were called Adam and Eve. The Bad Spirit became like a big snake or serpent and hid in the garden.

Adam and Eve did not know that he was there. They were listening to God for Him to tell them what to do. God said, 'I want you to be happy in this garden, and you may have it all, except one tree, which is Mine. It is covered with a fruit which I do not want you to eat.'

His promise that men were to enjoy all the good things that came out of the earth was the first one which God made to people. Later on, we shall hear of other promises He has made.

When the serpent heard God say this, he went and curled himself up by the tree and waited for Adam and Eve to come.

Eve arrived first, and the serpent started talking to her. 'Good morning,' he said. 'Wouldn't you like some of this nice fruit?'

'No, thank you,' said Eve. 'God said that we were not to eat it.'

'See how good it is,' said the serpent. 'Do have some. There is no harm in it.'

So Eve looked, and the fruit did seem very good. She hoped that God was not looking, and she put out her hand and took one.

Very soon Adam came along, and Eve said, 'Look what nice fruit I've got. Would you like to have some?'

She held the fruit out to Adam and he ate a piece too.

No sooner had they eaten it than God called to them and said, 'Adam and Eve, what have you done?'

They were both very much afraid, and they tried to pretend that it was not their fault.

Adam said, 'It was Eve's fault. She gave it to me.'
Eve said, 'It was the serpent's fault. He said that I could eat it.'
They both pointed their fingers at someone else, and not at themselves.

God said, 'Because you have done what you were told not to do, you cannot stay in the garden any longer.'
He told them that they must go out and dig and plant and grow food for themselves, with sweat and hard work. He also said that one day somebody would come who would bruise the serpent's head, and so conquer the evil that had been let loose in the world because of Adam and Eve's disobedience.
So Adam and Eve had to leave the garden and go and make a home in a new place.
They did not see the serpent again, but they could hear his voice telling them to be selfish and greedy and to say things that were not true. They could hear God's voice, too, when they listened; and then they had to decide which voice to obey.

The story of Adam and Eve is a very old story, but what happened to them is what happens to everyone. The Good Voice speaks to us and so does the Bad Voice and we have to choose which we will listen to.
In this book is the story of the battle in the world, the battle that goes on in people's hearts between what God wants and what the Bad Spirit wants, and how God's Plan for the world comes through people who listen and obey.

Noah

ADAM and Eve had children, and their children had children, and so on until there were a lot of people in the world. Some of them forgot about listening to God's voice and doing what He told them, and started doing what was wrong. They spoiled God's world.

However, there was a man called Noah, who still listened to God. One day God told him that it was going to rain for forty days and forty nights, and that there would be a great flood over the land. To keep Noah and his family safe, God showed him exactly how to build a boat, called an ark, which would be big enough for all his family and two of all the different animals and birds in the world as well.

Seven days before the rain came, God said to Noah that it was now time for them all to go inside the ark. Soon it started to pour with rain, and the land was covered with water. The ark floated on the floods and everyone inside was safe and dry.

It rained and rained for forty days and nights, and even after the rain had stopped no land could be seen for several months as everything was under water. All this time God was looking after Noah and his family and all the animals.

After seven months the ark suddenly floated on to the top of a mountain. There it rested safely until the water had dried up, and the animals were able to come out of the ark and find food for themselves. Noah and his family came out too, and one of the first things they did was to say 'Thank you' to God for the way He had looked after them.

Then God made another great promise. He told Noah that he and his family would be blessed and that they had been chosen to carry on God's Plan for the world. He said that He would never send another flood, and gave Noah a sign, so that men could always be reminded of His promise. God said, 'I have set My bow in the sky.' Every time we see a rainbow, we can remember this.

* * *

The story of Noah happened long ago, but learned men have found traces of the flood in different places.

Many people are puzzled by the bad things that happen in the world. Often they say it is God's fault. Sometimes they say they do not believe that God is really there, because if He were, He would not let things go wrong. God has never tried to make things easy for people. He has given them the chance to grow strong by learning to make the right decisions, and He has let them know all that they needed to know at any time if they listened to Him.

Noah was a man who believed that God had a plan; but none of the families round about understood this. When God warned him that the rain was coming and would sweep them all away if they were not prepared, he tried to warn his neighbours too. But they would not listen.

Noah and his family followed the plan which God gave them, and because of this they were not swept away in the flood.

Noah's family grew. His sons, Ham, Shem and Japheth, and their wives and children, settled in new homes. Their children grew up, and their children's children. As the years went by, they moved about from place to place to find new pastures for their flocks, until in the course of time we find one of them living in a town called Ur of the Chaldees; his name was Abram.

You can still visit Ur nowadays. Its ruins were dug up not so long ago. It lies in the banks of the river Euphrates in Iraq. The ruined remains of its temple rise up towards Heaven, with broad stairways leading from one to the other of the three storeys.

Abram who became Abraham

ABRAM, who started life in Ur of the Chaldees, belonged to one of those wandering families which moved from place to place with all their flocks and possessions. By the time he comes into this part of the story he was already an old man. He was seventy-five, and, with Sarah his wife, had moved to a place called Haran in Syria, right up north on the Euphrates near what is now Turkey. They had no children, and this made them sad; but they had long ago given up the idea of having any.

One day God called Abram and said to him, 'I want you to move from here into another country, because I am going to make a great nation from your family. You shall have a son who will be the father of many people.'

A nation is a whole country full of people, and that was a surprising thing to say to an old man who had no children at all. But God's Plan always works through people who do what He says. So when He said to Abram, 'You must go to another country now,' Abram obeyed. And when God told him that he and Sarah would have a son, Abram believed that it would happen. By believing God, Abram showed everyone who came after him that the greatest thing a person can do is to trust God's promises.

God made yet another of His great promises. He said, 'I am the Almighty God. Live knowing that I am always with you, and be perfect. If you do, I will make you the father of many nations. And it will be one of the children who come after you who will bring something quite new to everybody in the world.' Then He gave Abram signs of this promise. One was that He changed his name from Abram, which means 'Great Father', to Abraham, which means 'Father of Millions'.

So for the rest of the story he is Abraham. But he must have found it hard to go on believing, because even after this promise many years went by before the baby was born. During that time Abraham travelled a long way to the new country about which God had told him.

In those days it was hard for pèople to understand that there could be a real God whom they could not see or feel. Not everyone can understand this today. But seeing and feeling are not the most important part of knowing God. Hearing is even more important; and God chose Abraham and his family to learn this and to teach it to the world.

The far country to which he went was the country which, many years later, God was to give to his descendants—that is to say, his children, grandchildren and great-great-great-many-great-grandchildren. In fact, God had chosen Abraham to be the many-times-great-grandfather of a Special Person, whom He was going to send into the world hundreds of years later.

Believing and doing what God says is called 'having faith'. For people to have faith is part of God's Plan, because then they obey Him even when they do not quite understand. When Noah built the ark, he did not know that Abraham would be born into his family many years later. When Abraham moved into a new country to start a new family, he did not know what God's Plan was for that family. But when he died as a very old man, he knew that he had done the part of the plan which God meant him to do.

When Abraham and Sarah's son was born, they called him Isaac, which means 'Laughter', because Sarah had laughed when she heard that she was to have a baby. Abraham and Sarah loved Isaac very much, more than anything in the world. He grew up very happily with his two old parents.

In those days, when people wanted to please God, to do honour to Him and worship Him, they used to kill an animal and burn it on a little table of stones, called an altar. Sometimes it was a sheep or a goat which they would have liked to have kept for themselves. They felt that this was a way of giving it to God.

Abraham had often done this. It was called making a sacrifice. One day he was thinking about God and what he could give Him, when it seemed to him that God said, 'You must give me Isaac as a sacrifice.'

This was a very hard thing for Abraham to do, because he only knew of one way of giving anything to God, and that was by killing it. He felt that God must be wanting him to make a sacrifice of Isaac by killing him. That was a terrible thought. But he was so absolutely sure that he must do just what God said, that he started to make preparations for sacrificing his son.

He said to Isaac, 'I am going to make a sacrifice, and you must come and help me.' So Isaac went with his father. When he saw that there was no animal, he was puzzled, and said, 'But, Father, where is the lamb for the sacrifice?' Abraham did not want to say what he meant to do, and he replied, 'God will give us one.' He went sadly to the hill where he had decided to build the altar. Then, just at the moment when he thought he would have to kill Isaac, God called to him and said, 'Abraham, Abraham,' and Abraham said, 'Here I am.'

God said, 'Do not hurt your son. I see how much you love Me, because you were ready to give him to Me in this way. But I do not want you to kill him.'

Abraham was overjoyed when he heard this. But he had the idea of a sacrifice very firmly in his head. So God told him that if he looked around he would see a sheep caught in a bush, and he could kill that and make a sacrifice of it.

Abraham sacrificed the sheep and took Isaac home again. He gave him to God in quite a different way, by helping him to do what God said, and to have faith and to be obedient.

This idea of a sacrifice was an important one to Abraham's whole family. They felt that they must give something to God that was precious, and also perfect, and give it in such a way that they could not get it back.

They felt, too, about the sacrifice that it was a way of being forgiven, and that by shedding the blood of a lamb they did not have to die themselves for having done wrong.

All the way through the story of Abraham and his people you will find this thought of the death of a lamb, and the equally important idea that the lamb had to be absolutely perfect, and have nothing wrong with it.

Abraham had another son called Ishmael, whose mother was Hagar, an Egyptian. Ishmael became the father of all the Arabs, who are cousins of the Jews.

Jacob

WHEN Isaac grew up, he married a young girl called Rebecca, and you can read the story of how he met her in Genesis, the first book of the Bible. They had twin sons called Jacob and Esau, and the story goes on through Jacob's family.

Although God had chosen Abraham and his children and their children for a special part of His Plan, it does not mean that they were naturally good people, or better than anyone else. Fortunately, God does not choose people because they are good, but because He loves them, and because they can listen and obey and become different. Anyone who listens will find that he or she has been chosen for a particular part in God's Plan too.

Abraham's descendants were often very difficult and quarrelsome. They could be fierce and unkind and play horrid tricks on each other. For example, towards the end of Isaac's life, he went blind and wanted to bless Esau, his elder son. But Jacob put on Esau's clothes and made himself feel like Esau. In this way he got Isaac to give him the special blessing which should have gone to the elder brother Esau. When Esau found out, he tried to kill Jacob, who had to leave home and go far away.

One night, when he was travelling alone, he had a dream. God told Jacob in this dream what He had told his grandfather Abraham many years before. This was that He had a plan for their family, and was going to give them a country to live in, and that many blessings would come to the world through them.

Although Jacob was not always honest, and although he played a bad trick on his brother, he nevertheless tried to follow the great plan of God for himself and his whole family. For this reason, God stayed close to him. God also told him he should have a new name, Israel, which means 'A Prince close to God'. From that time, all Jacob's family (he had twelve sons) and their children and children's children were known as the Children of Israel. This was to show that they were a people who specially belonged to God.

After a time God began to speak to Jacob about his brother Esau, with whom he had quarrelled so many years ago, and Jacob decided to go to where his brother lived and make peace with him. So he and his family all went back, and Jacob and Esau made friends again, and were able to be with their old father Isaac in the last years of his life, as friends and not enemies.

Joseph

THERE came a time when Jacob's sons were nearly all grown up, except the two youngest, whose names were Joseph and Benjamin. Their work as a family each day was to look after all the flocks which belonged to Jacob, to protect them from robbers and from wild animals. Jacob was proud of all his sons, but the one he loved the most was Joseph. He was always doing special things for Joseph, and once he gave him a beautiful coat with many colours in it, because he loved him so much.

This made Joseph's big brothers very jealous. They wished their father would give them beautiful coats too, and they began to hate Joseph. Everything he did made them cross, and they listened to the Bad Voice and not to God.

One day Joseph said to them, 'I had a queer dream last night. I dreamt that we were making sheaves of corn in a field, and that when we had made them, all your sheaves stood up and bowed to mine.'

His brothers said they thought it was a very silly dream, but it made them angry to think of their sheaves bowing to his, even in a dream.

Then Joseph had another dream. It was that the sun and moon and eleven stars came and bowed to him. He told his brothers about it. This time even his father was quite cross, perhaps because he did not think that such a young boy ought to be dreaming about so many things bowing to him.

Perhaps, too, his father thought he was having so many dreams because he was not working hard enough, so one day he said to him, 'Your brothers are looking after the sheep at a place a little way from here. Go and see if they need any help and come back and let me know.'

His brothers saw him coming and said, 'Look, here comes the dreamer! What shall we do with him?'

And they decided to kill him.

But one of the brothers, whose name was Reuben, said, 'No, that would be very wrong. Let us put him in this hole here and leave him.' Reuben thought that by doing this he could keep Joseph safe. Then, when the others were not looking, he would be able to take him home. Though the others agreed, it did not happen as Reuben had hoped. When his back was turned, perhaps when he had gone to fetch some water—the story does not say exactly—some travellers passed by on the way to Egypt. The other brothers stopped them and asked them if they would buy Joseph and take him with them.

The travellers did so and took Joseph away and sold him as a slave to a rich Egyptian called Potiphar. His brothers went home and told Jacob that he was dead. They dipped his beautiful coloured coat in goat's blood and showed it to their father, saying that Joseph had been killed by a wild animal.

God, however, loved Joseph and looked after him and told him what to do. He became loved and trusted by his master, Potiphar, who put him in charge of his whole household. Joseph still had strange dreams, and one day the king, Pharaoh, had a strange dream too about seven very fine fat cows which came out of the river, and seven thin hungry cows which came after them and ate them up.

The king wondered what it meant, and sent for Joseph to explain it. Joseph said that the fat cows meant seven years during which food would grow plentifully, and the people would have all they needed. These years of plenty would be followed by seven years when there was little to eat. The crops would not grow for lack of water, and all the food of the seven good years would be eaten by the seven bad or thin years which would follow.

'What shall we do then?' asked the king.

Joseph replied, 'I think the best thing to do would be to build great barns during the full and good years, and we can put all the extra corn that we do not need into them. Then when the thin years come we shall have something to live on.'

The king thought this was a good idea, and he told Joseph to build the barns and fill them, to make sure that people had enough to eat when the bad times came. He put him in charge of all the food in Egypt.

So Joseph was able to keep the country from starving. The bad times came, as he had said, and everyone came to Joseph, and he sold them corn.

Meanwhile the people in the countries around about were desperate. They had not built barns, and had eaten all the food they had had in the full years. Among them was Joseph's own family, his old father and all his brothers.

One day old Jacob said to them, 'Why not go to Egypt? There is corn in Egypt. Take money and presents to the Egyptians. I hear the head man is wise and good, and he might sell you some corn.'

So the brothers loaded their camels with presents and set off for

Egypt. They left behind them their father, and their youngest brother Benjamin.

After a long journey they reached Egypt. They asked to see the king's adviser, and Joseph was told that there were some men from a far country waiting to see him. You can imagine his surprise when his brothers were brought to him! He recognised them, though they did not know him, because he had only been a boy when they saw him last, and now he had become a man in Egypt, and was dressed like an Egyptian prince.

They bowed to him, for he was a great man; but none of them remembered their little brother's dream of so long ago when their sheaves had bowed to his.

Joseph looked at all his brothers and he loved them in spite of everything. He longed to have news of his father and his brother Benjamin, but he did not tell them who he was. He pretended to be cross with them, and said he thought they were enemies. He asked them a lot of questions about their home, and their father, as if he did not know anything at all. And he got them to tell him that they had a younger brother who had not come with them.

Then he said, 'I will only believe that you are not enemies if you go home and bring your brother back here. One of you must stay here

with me as a prisoner, so that I can be sure you will come back, but I will let him go as soon as you bring your youngest brother.'

The brothers were sad when they heard this. They said they were sure their father would not let Benjamin come; but Joseph said they must do as he told them, or he would not give them food. So one brother called Simeon stayed, and the others went back for Benjamin.

The Brothers Find Each Other Again

JOSEPH told his servants to give his brothers the corn they needed, and they started for home. But on the first evening, when they stopped to rest and opened their bags, they were surprised to find in them the money they had given for the corn. This was because Joseph had not wanted to take money from them, and had told his servants to return it in this way.

All the same, the brothers' hearts were heavy when they got home, because they knew they had to tell old Jacob, their father, about Simeon and Benjamin.

Poor Jacob felt that his heart was nearly broken. 'Joseph has gone,' he said. 'Simeon has gone. Now Benjamin is going and I am sure I shall never see him again.' But he realised that if he did not let Benjamin go, they might not get any more food. So he gave his permission and the brothers all went back together.

When they arrived, Joseph had a big feast made ready to welcome them. He invited them all to come, and Simeon was given back to them. He asked after their old father, but still without saying that Jacob was his father too. Then he looked round till he saw Benjamin.

'Is this your younger brother,' he asked, 'the one you told me about?' They said it was.

Joseph was so happy to see Benjamin again that he felt he was going to cry, so he went away quickly and did cry a little when no one was looking. When he felt better he came back, and they had the feast. He always gave Benjamin a much bigger helping than any of the others. But he still did not tell them who he was.

When the time came for them all to go home, Joseph told his

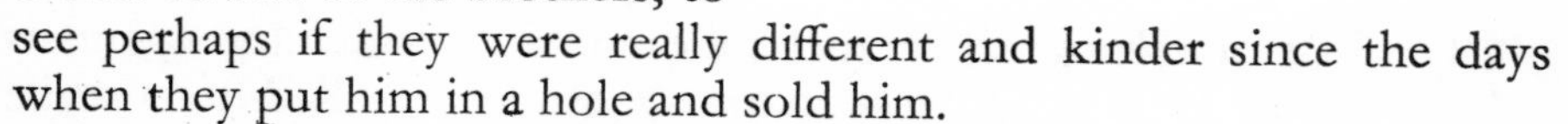

servants to fill the brothers' sacks with food and again to put the corn money back, but also to put his own silver drinking cup in Benjamin's sack.

This was not in order to be kind, but so that he might make a sort of test of his brothers, to see perhaps if they were really different and kinder since the days when they put him in a hole and sold him.

After they had gone a little way he sent messengers after them who said, 'You have stolen our master's silver cup. We shall have to look through all your things to see who has it.'

The brothers were very hurt that anyone should think they had stolen the cup of the great lord who had been so kind to them, but the messengers said they must search everywhere. Of course, when they looked, there the cup was in Benjamin's sack.

The messengers took them back again to Egypt. When they arrived they said they had no idea how the cup had come to be in Benjamin's sack, and they begged Joseph not to punish him.

'You can do anything to any of us,' they said, 'but we have promised our father to bring Benjamin back safely.'

They told him how their father had had another son, who had been 'lost', as they said, and whatever happened to the rest of them Benjamin must be allowed to go home.

Then Joseph knew that the one thing they all wanted was that no harm should come to their youngest brother. He saw that they were not jealous of their father's love for him, and that they would not hurt Benjamin as they had hurt himself. He sent away the Egyptian servants. When he was alone with his brothers he told them who he was, and all that had happened to him since they sold him as a slave many years ago.

He asked them all to come and live with him in Egypt. 'God,' he said, 'has allowed all these things to happen, so that when the bad times came I could save our family.'

So Joseph's family, his old father Jacob, his brothers and all their families moved into Egypt. They were safe and happy there, and Pharaoh, the king, looked after them for Joseph's sake.

Moses

JOSEPH and his brothers had children and grandchildren, and as the family grew larger, Joseph looked after them all. After a while the kind Pharaoh died, and in time Joseph and his brothers died too. Other kings, also called Pharaoh, came to the throne, and many years went by.

More and more children were born, but the later Pharaohs were no longer friendly towards the people of Israel, as they had been towards Joseph. Nor were they at all pleased to have so many Israelites living in their country.

There came a time when one of the Pharaohs gave orders that they should become the Egyptians' servants and do all the hard work. This Pharaoh was afraid that if they were allowed to have houses and gardens and cattle of their own, they might come to think that the country belonged to them. They might even become more powerful than the Egyptians themselves.

Pharaoh decided that he would not allow the Israelites to own anything. He was hard and strict and often cruel. In spite of this, the babies kept being born, and there were still more Israelites. This worried Pharaoh, even though they were now his slaves. One day he gave an order that the nurses, who went to look after the babies when they had just been born, should kill the boys, to stop the family of Israel from growing.

The nurses were women who feared God, and they did not obey Pharaoh. When he asked them why they had not obeyed his orders, they made excuses. They were afraid to tell the king that they had not even tried to obey him.

There was one mother who had a baby boy, and when he was about three months old she decided that it was no longer safe to keep him in the house. She made a basket of rushes covered with tar, to keep the water out, put the baby to sleep in it and set it floating on the water among the rushes. The baby's sister, Miriam, watched from a little way off, to see what would happen.

After a while, Pharaoh's daughter, the princess, came to the river to bathe. She was very much surprised to see this basket floating in the water and asked one of her maids to fetch it. The maid went into the water and brought the basket back. She opened the lid and looked inside, and there was a baby sound asleep. As they looked at him, he woke up and began to cry.

'Oh, the poor little thing,' said the princess. 'This must be one of the slaves' babies. What can we do for it?' She knew what her father felt about the Israelites. If he saw her with the baby and knew where it came from, he would certainly take it away and have it killed.

Just then Miriam, who had been listening from behind the rushes, came up.

She did not say she was the baby's sister. She said, 'Shall I go and find a nurse to help you with the baby?'

To her great delight the princess said, 'Yes, please do.'

Miriam ran home to her mother and told her what had happened, and they came back together.

The princess, who did not know this was the baby's mother, said, 'Will you look after this child for me? I will pay you for doing it, and I should like to bring him up as my son.' So his mother took the baby home again. She let people know that she was looking after him for the princess, and the princess called the baby 'Moses', which means 'pulled out of the water'.

God Calls Moses

MOSES was brought up as the son of the princess. But the rest of his people had to go on working for the Egyptians and were often badly treated.

Once Moses went out and saw one of the Egyptians beating an Israelite. He was so angry that he killed the Egyptian. He thought no one was looking, but somehow the news reached Pharaoh. To escape his anger, Moses ran away to an Arab country called Midian, where he stayed with a man called Jethro, and looked after his sheep. Jethro was one of Ishmael's descendants, and Moses married one of his daughters.

One day Moses was out with the sheep when he saw what looked to him like a bush burning. He went to see what it was, and when he looked a little closer he saw that though there were flames all over the bush, it was not being burnt up. This seemed curious, so he looked again. As he looked, God spoke to him out of the middle of the flames, saying, 'Moses, Moses,' and Moses answered, 'Here I am.'

Then God said, 'Come no nearer and take off your shoes.' In that hot country people take their shoes off to be polite to God, just as men in other countries take their hats off when they go into church or want to be polite to people.

Moses felt quite afraid that God should speak to him like this, and hid his face.

Then God said how much He had been thinking of all the children of Israel who were in Egypt. He had heard and seen how unhappy they were, and He wanted to take them to a new land which should belong to them.

'I want them to go to a good land,' said God, 'a large land, flowing with milk and honey.' That meant that it was not a desert, but that good and satisfying food could grow there and the people of Israel would always have enough to eat. Then He went on to say that He wanted Moses to go to Pharaoh and ask him to let the people go.

Moses said, 'Who am I to go to Pharaoh and bring the people of Israel out of Egypt?' God answered, 'I will certainly be with you, and

to show you that I mean what I say, I promise that you shall bring the people from Egypt back to this hill where we are now standing, and they shall pray to Me here.'

'But will the people believe that you have sent me?' asked Moses. 'Besides, I am bad at speaking. I shall not know how to talk to Pharaoh.'

Then God said, 'What about your brother Aaron? He is good at speaking. He shall speak for you, and I will give him and you the words to say.'

Aaron was still in Egypt, but God spoke to him there, and told him to go and meet Moses in the wilderness. So Aaron set off, and the two brothers met on the mountain where Moses had seen the burning bush. Moses told Aaron all that God had told him. Then they went back to Egypt and gathered all the chief men of Israel together to tell them what had happened. Aaron did the talking, as God had said he should, and the people knew that they had not been forgotten, and that God had a plan for them.

Moses and Pharaoh

GOD said, 'You must say everything that I tell you, and your brother Aaron shall speak to Pharaoh, and tell him to let the people of Israel go out of his land. Very likely Pharaoh will ask you to show him some sign, and if he does, Aaron must throw his stick down on the ground and it will become a serpent.'

So Moses and Aaron did what they were told, and when Pharaoh asked them for a sign, Aaron threw his stick down, and, sure enough, it became a serpent.

Then Pharaoh asked his own magicians to use their magic and to turn their rods into serpents. They did this, but Aaron's rod ate up all the others.

Instead of Pharaoh letting the people go, he only made them work harder.

So God told Moses and Aaron to say that many terrible things would happen in Egypt if Pharaoh still refused. He did refuse, and, one after another, things started to go wrong in the country.

The water went bad so that people could not drink it. There was what is called a plague of frogs, which means that swarms of frogs came out of the river. Wherever people went, frogs were jumping and crawling under their feet.

Then there came a plague of insects, flying and creeping everywhere. First one plague came and then another. Each time Pharaoh said he would let the people go, and then God would let the plague stop. But when things seemed better, Pharaoh would change his mind and say that the Israelites could not go after all.

God is always showing His children new things, but sometimes people stand in the way of His Plan. This time it was Pharaoh who stood in the way. As Pharaoh and the Egyptians were keeping God's people, God said He would take some of their people. He said He would take the eldest boy in every family, and the eldest animal in every family. In this way Pharaoh would really understand that he could not keep what did not belong to him.

Meanwhile God told Moses to prepare the people for the journey out of Egypt. He also told him to warn Pharaoh of what was going to happen; but still he would not let the people go.

Moses told the Israelites to start getting ready. God had said they must have a special supper, each family in its own house, which would be their last supper in Egypt. He said that at midnight He would send an angel to fetch the Egyptian children.

This special evening has been called the Passover, because the angel of God passed over the children of the Israelites. In each family a lamb was killed instead.

They had the meal and were ready to go. As they waited, the angel came and took the Egyptian children.

When Pharaoh found that this had happened, and that his own child was one of those who had died, he decided he could not keep the people of Israel any longer. He called for Moses and Aaron, there and then in the middle of the night, and told them to go at once, and all the Egyptians said the same thing. They could not hurry them out of the country quickly enough.

Moses and His People Leave Egypt

MOSES and Aaron went back to their people who were ready waiting. They told them that the moment had come to start, even though it was still night. Off they all went into the desert with their children and their animals, and everything that they could carry. It was a good thing that they had started the moment God told them to, because they had not been gone long when Pharaoh changed his mind again.

He said, 'Why have we let the people of Israel go from being our servants?' And he took six hundred chariots as well as soldiers and horsemen, and went after the Israelites to bring them back.

They saw Pharaoh coming, and immediately began to blame Moses, saying, 'Why have you brought us here to be killed in the desert? We might just as well have died in Egypt.' But Moses said, 'Fear not, for

God will save you. God will fight for you if you will be quiet and watch His Plan work out.'

By this time the people had come to what is called the Red Sea, and there was no way across it. There were neither boats nor a bridge, and the Egyptians were coming up so fast behind that the people found it hard to believe that they could be saved.

But God had a plan for them. He told Moses to stretch his hand out over the sea, and a dry path would appear over which they could pass. Moses did so, and God sent a strong wind which pushed back the waters, and the people were able to walk across safely. The water seemed like a wall on either side of them.

God had already given Moses two signs to guide him. One was a fiery pillar in the sky at night, the other was a pillar of cloud in the sky by day. These were to go ahead of the people of Israel and show them which way to go. The Egyptians were coming nearer all the time while the Israelites were going across the dry path over the sea. God put a cloud behind the people of Israel, so that the Egyptians could not see them and catch up with them. Everything became dark and misty on the Egyptian side, but the side where Moses and his people were was light, and they came across safely.

By this time the Egyptians had managed to get through the cloud, and had come to the edge of the sea. They started across too, but the waters came together again, and though the Egyptians with their horses and chariots struggled to reach the other side, the water covered them and they were all drowned.

Miriam, Moses' sister, sang a song of thanks to God for bringing her and her people safely over the Red Sea.

However, their difficulties were only just beginning. Though they had been ill-treated and unhappy in Egypt, in another way they had been safe. They had never had to decide anything for themselves, since their masters had always told them what to do. They had not always had a great deal to eat and drink, but on the whole they had had enough. Now here they were in the desert with no houses, sometimes no water and no food. What they did have was the promise that God would give them all they needed, if they would listen and obey.

It really meant that from now onwards, although they would be free from doing what their masters told them, they also had to make up their own minds whether they were going to obey God's voice or the Devil's. The next part of the story tells how God tried to make them understand this.

Early Days in the Wilderness

THREE days after the Israelites had crossed the Red Sea, they ran out of water. They must have brought some with them, but it was gone, and they did not find any wells in the desert. They became very thirsty and this made them angry. They were even angrier when they came to a well where the water tasted so bitter that they could not drink it. They all grumbled and said to Moses, 'What are we going to drink?'

Moses was almost the only person in that great crowd of people who really knew how to listen to God, and who knew that there was no need to be afraid if things seemed to go wrong. Even Aaron did not know as much about listening as Moses, because it was his part to do the talking, while Moses would tell Aaron what God wanted him to say.

So it was again Moses who asked God what to do. God answered that there was a certain kind of tree near the pool which, if thrown into the water, would take away the bitter taste.

Moses threw the tree into the water, and the people drank it and found it had become fresh.

Moses then spoke to them all and said, 'If you will diligently (that means carefully and honestly) listen to the voice of the Lord your God, and do what is right, and pay attention to all He says, and obey all His laws, none of the diseases that came upon the Egyptians will come upon you, for it is the Lord who heals you.'

The people must have understood that and listened to the voice of God, because after a while they came to a place called Elim where there were no fewer than twelve wells of water and seventy palm trees. There they had shade and water, and they all camped by the wells for a while and rested.

When they had rested, they moved on through the desert, or the wilderness as it was also called. They travelled until they had eaten the last bits of food they had brought with them. They had brought a certain amount of flour and honey and vegetables, but now that was gone and they were very hungry.

THE JOURNEYINGS OF THE ISRAELITES
JERICHO
CANAAN
MT. NEBO
EGYPT
MT SINAI.
N
W
E
S

They wished they could get to the Promised Land and settle down. They had been travelling in the wilderness for six weeks, and felt sure they must be going to reach their new country soon; but God's Plan was not just that they should move quickly from one place to another. The important thing was for them to get to know and understand Him.

Moses knew this. He knew that he had been called to teach the people about God, to show them how much God loved and cared for them, and what the difference was between being slaves who obeyed their masters, and free people who obeyed God.

The Israelites had been slaves for so many years that it was going to take them a long time to understand what Moses was trying to teach them. It was true that God had brought them over the Red Sea, and made the water good to drink, but the people found it hard to remember these things when some new difficulty came along. Now it was hunger which frightened them.

Again they grumbled against Moses and complained about having left Egypt. They forgot their unhappiness there, and only remembered the fact that they had always known what was going to happen next. Each day they would get up and go to work, they would get some food and even though they might be beaten, they knew they would go to bed again.

Here in the desert they never knew what would happen next. They did not know how far they had to go, nor if they would find food or water. They only knew that Moses had said that God would look after them. Now, because they were hungry, it seemed as if God were not doing this.

Moses prayed and asked God what to do, and God told him about the food He had planned.

He said, 'I will rain bread from heaven for you, and the people must go out and gather a certain amount each morning. In the evening I will send birds called quails.'

So Moses asked Aaron to call the people together and tell them this.

It happened as God had said. In the evening a flock of quails came flying through the air over the desert to the Israelites' camp, and they were able to catch these quite easily and cook them.

In the morning when the dew had gone from the ground they found the bread God had promised them. It was not quite what we know as bread. It was more like very fine flour. It covered the ground like a white powder which the people could gather and put into jars.

Something like this comes to this day in hot parts of the world in certain seasons. It tastes like honey, and delicious sweets are made with it.

God said very clearly that nobody was to take more than he or she needed for one day. Everybody, He said, could take a certain definite amount, and no one was to try and take enough for two days.

However, one or two people did take more than they needed. Either they were greedy, or else they were afraid there might not be another lot next morning, and it would be as well to be on the safe side. When these people went and looked into their sacks the next morning, they found that the food, which they called manna, had gone bad.

God wanted the people to learn to believe what He said. When He said there would be manna next day, there would be manna next day. When He said they must not be greedy, they were not to be greedy.

There was only one day on which they were allowed to gather a double quantity. That was on the sixth day of the week, because the seventh was God's day, the day of rest. On this day they were not to work at picking up the manna. On the day when God allowed them to have a double quantity, it did not go bad, but was as good on the second day as it had been on the first.

The Years of Training

SO the Israelites journeyed through the wilderness. It took a very long time. This was partly because they had to walk all the way, and also because it always takes longer to move a big crowd of people than one or two. Often they had to stop and rest for a few days or longer. One day they had gone as far as they could, and Moses and Aaron felt it was time to stop. They looked round for a well, but could not find one.

The people were tired and refused to go any farther. They were also very thirsty. Once more they became angry with Moses for having made them come away from Egypt into the wilderness.

'Why have you brought us here?' they said. 'We are all going to die of thirst.' Moses felt almost in despair about their grumbles and disobedience, but as he always did when things were difficult, he asked God what to do.

'Oh, Lord,' he said, 'what can I do with these people? They are just about to throw stones at me, they are so angry.'

God answered and said, 'Go and stand before the people. Take some of the chief men with you and take the staff with which you made the waters of the sea divide. I will be with you. Strike the great rock which is standing there, and water will come flowing out for the people to drink.'

Moses did as God said. A great stream of water came flowing out. Once more the people trusted Moses and believed that he really heard God talk to him.

But they found it terribly hard always to believe that even when things were difficult God had a plan. People today still find this hard too.

Another thing they did not find easy was getting on with each other, which is also just like people today. So Moses decided to stay where the water was, and try to help them.

Every day, he said, he would be sitting in a certain place at certain times. Anyone who was angry about anything or with someone else, or who did not understand something, could come and talk to him about it.

After a while so many people wanted to ask his advice that he could not get away at all. He would sit there from early in the morning till late at night talking to each one in turn. It was much more than he could manage on his own, and he was exhausted.

Just then his wife's father, Jethro, came to see him. He brought Moses' wife, and two little boys, who had been left with their grandfather while Moses was bringing the Israelites out of Egypt. When Jethro saw Moses spending the whole day talking to people, he saw how tired it was making him. One day he said, 'This is too much for you to do by yourself. You will wear yourself out.'

Moses said, 'But the people come to me to ask me about God. I have to tell them. So many of them know nothing of Him.'

'That is true,' said Jethro. 'You are meant to teach them, but you cannot do it alone. You must train other people to help you. If you choose some of the wisest men, and let them work with you, they will learn how to do it too.'

Moses felt that this was a good plan, and he chose men to help him as his wife's father had suggested. He found he still had to decide the most difficult things himself, but soon the men he had chosen became able to answer a lot of questions without asking him.

Soon after this, Jethro went home again. He had helped Moses to see that no one person can do everything quite alone, and that even the wisest person needs others to help him. In this way more people learn and have the chance to become wiser together.

God Gives His Laws

AFTER a while Moses and his friends felt it was time for the people to move on. God told him that He had new lessons to teach them.

So the people packed up their tents and went to camp in front of a mountain called Mount Sinai. Here God gave Moses another of the great promises in His Plan for men.

He called Moses and said, 'Tell the people that they are My people, and that if they do My will, I will make them a holy nation.' When Moses told them that, the people said, 'We will do what God says.'

Then God called Moses again and said, 'Come up into the mountain and I will speak to you and give you laws for the people.' The Bible says that a thick cloud came down on the mountain and all the people saw it. They watched Moses go up through the cloud.

The first thing God said was, 'I am the Lord thy God. Thou shalt have no other gods before Me.'

In those days people thought there were many different gods—rain gods, and earth gods and sun gods. They thought that they were mostly rather cruel, and that men must try not to make them angry, but make sacrifices to them to keep them in a good temper.

God told Moses that He was not like these gods. No one could make a statue of Him, and no one must even try. Whenever we make a statue of God, we make Him like us, small and foolish. What God wants is to make us more and more like Him. God told Moses many more things about the way to live, and how to behave one to another. Moses wrote them down on large flat stones, as they had no paper in those days.

All this took a long time, and after Moses had been away for many days, the people began to wonder what had happened to him, and they became impatient. They went to Aaron and said, 'Where is this man Moses?' Then they asked Aaron to make them a god which they could see. Aaron, who felt rather lost without Moses, told them to bring all their golden ornaments so that he could melt them down. From the melted gold Aaron made a golden calf. The people forgot about Moses and how they had said they would do what God wanted. They danced and sang and prayed to the statue of the calf, and became very excited and noisy.

Just then Moses came back. Coming down the hill, he heard all the noise and shouting. As he came nearer he saw what was happening.

Poor Moses! He was heartbroken and angry, so much so that he threw down the great stones with the laws of God written on them, and they broke. Then he went to Aaron and asked what had happened. 'How did they come to make you do such a dreadful thing?' asked Moses.

Aaron answered, 'Do not be so angry. I could see they meant trouble, so I made them give me their gold ornaments and I melted them down and out came this calf.'

Moses realised how hard it was going to be for his wild people to understand about God. It was going to take a long time for them to learn to listen and obey. He punished the men who were most to

blame. Then he went back to the mountain and prayed that God would forgive the people and go on teaching them about Himself. God renewed His promises to Moses and told him He would lead them on into their new country. But He was very firm that they must change their ways and put Him first, otherwise He would not stay with them. He told Moses to cut two new tablets of stones so that the laws He had given him could be written on them again. And He came closer than ever to Moses and talked with him like a friend. But He warned Moses that the people must give all of their hearts to Him and have no other God but Himself.

So Moses took the rewritten laws back to his people. The Bible says that they saw that his face shone after he had been talking and listening to God. By this time the people were sorry for what they had done, and they were frightened too. As one way of showing that they were really sorry, Moses invited them all to help to make a beautiful great tent as a travelling temple, or church, which would remind them about God, and help them to see that He was ready to go everywhere with them.

The laws were a guide to the people as to how God wanted them to live. Until that time they had lived without proper laws, or with other people's laws. Now God gave them a clear plan as to how He wanted them to live and work. He showed them that all laws and rules begin with Him, and with obedience to Him. That comes first of all. They were to worship Him only, and do what He said in everything.

Every man was to love his neighbour as much as himself. They were to keep one day in seven as a special day to rest and worship God. They were to honour their parents. No one must kill anyone. Husbands and wives must stay together. No one must steal, or even be jealous of anything anyone else had. No one must say unkind or untrue things about any other people.

These laws which are known as the Ten Commandments, and further precepts such as what we call the Golden Rule that 'every man should love his neighbour as himself', sound simple to us, but were very new to many of the Israelites. They have guided men and shown them how to live for thousands of years since Moses' time. God said to the people, what we need to remember too, that laws can be written on stone for us to see, but they also need to be written on our wills and hearts, so that we think about them, and they become part of us, and we obey them.

How Moses Disobeyed

THERE were many tribes living all around who believed in different gods who were supposed to allow their people to do things which the Israelites knew that God Himself would not permit. These people tried in every way to get the Israelites to do things which God had told them were wrong.

God kept the Israelites in the wilderness for many years before He let them go into the new land which He had promised them, because that land was full of men with wrong ideas. He wanted to be sure that the Israelites were so strong in their understanding of what was right that they would stick to it, and not copy the bad ideas in the country to which they were going.

They had many adventures and learnt many lessons. There was a time when they again asked for meat to eat, and God again sent some quails. The people were greedy and ate too much, because they found it hard to believe that there would be enough for everyone. There were times too when they thought they knew best, and went and fought battles which God had not told them to fight. Many times they turned against Moses, until one day Moses lost his temper with them, which seems to have been the only time God was angry with him.

It happened this way. The people were again short of water, and once more they turned on Moses and said they wished they could go back to Egypt. So Moses and Aaron prayed and asked God's help. He told Moses to go with Aaron and gather the people together in front of a big rock. Then Moses was to speak to the rock, and water would come from it for the Israelites and their animals.

Instead of this, Moses took his stick and said very angrily, 'Hear now, ye rebels, must we fetch you water out of this rock?' Then he hit the rock with his rod. This was not at all what God had told him to do. For one thing, He had said, 'Speak to the rock', and not 'Hit it', and for another thing Moses made it seem as if it was he who was making the water come, and not God. In spite of this, God let the water flow because the people needed it. But afterwards He spoke sternly to Moses, and told him that because of this disobedience he would not be allowed to take the Israelites into the Promised Land nor would Aaron, but that they must train the people in obedience all the rest of the time they were in the wilderness.

At the same time God made another great promise. Some of the things He said in it were that His word was always going to be 'very close to the people, in their mouths, in their hearts, so that they could obey it'. He also said that He would give them new hearts, 'So that they could love him with all their heart and with all their soul.'

God said that a man called Joshua was to take the place of Moses and Aaron, and lead the people into the Promised Land. Joshua had been trained by Moses from the time he was a boy. Before Moses died, he told Joshua he was to be the next leader, and he also told him and the people of Israel about the dangers that would lie ahead of them in the land to which they were going. He warned them that they would again want to have man-made gods, because it was easier to believe in something they could see. He told them they would be wiser to stick together, and not have too much to do with the people of the new land, who had bad ideas and bad ways.

Moses reminded them of all that God had done for them. He tried to write down all that they had learnt together in the wilderness. He knew that he could not stay with them for ever, and that he must have faith, like Abraham, that God would lead the people each step of the way through men whom He would send to help them. They would probably make a lot of mistakes; but even if they forgot God, God would not forget them. He told them that Joshua was going to lead them and look after them from then on. When he had done everything he felt God meant him to do for his people, he went up into a high mountain, and God showed him the Promised Land; then he died and went to be with God, for he was very old. Joshua took his place.

Joshua

THE first thing God said to Joshua was, 'Be brave.' It was not going to be at all easy to lead a lot of people who were always trying to get their own way. Moses had been with them for so long that, however bad they were, in the end they would listen to him. But Joshua had nothing to go on, except the fact that God had called him.

Strangely enough, the first thing he had to do was to take them across a river, just as Moses had taken them across the Red Sea when they came out of Egypt. There was no bridge and no way over. But God told Joshua He would make a dry place where they could cross, as He had done years before.

Probably there was hardly anyone left who remembered Egypt, for many years had passed since then. There was a completely new generation of people, most of them born in the wilderness. They had not been slaves, nor had they ever had any homes, or anything to depend on but God; and now God was going to give them a home and a country and everything they needed.

So you would have thought that they were going to be very happy. And, indeed, things went well to begin with. It is true that the people who already lived in Canaan (which was the name of the Promised Land) did not want the Israelites to come and live there too, and fought against them. The Canaanites were pagan tribes who still thought that there were a great many different gods, and the Israelites thought that the best thing they could do was to get rid of them. They knew it would be hard to stick together and keep their faith, so they took rough-and-ready ways of having the country to themselves.

They defeated the Canaanites, moved into the country and took it over. They divided it up between the different families, and settled down.

Now that the Israelites were safely settled in Canaan, they were sure that they would do everything God wanted, and Joshua looked after them all and cared for them till he became a very old man. When he knew he must leave his people, he called them together, and explained all that happened since they left Egypt, and even before that. He told them how God had called Abraham and Isaac and Moses, and how He had brought them out of Egypt and given them a new land of their own.

Joshua told them how important it was that they should go on obeying God, and not the man-made gods of the people who lived round about. He said, 'Choose you this day whom you will serve.' All the people said, 'Of course we shall obey God. He has done so much for us, looked after us and given us this land.'

Joshua told them very clearly that they could not obey God and at the same time pray to the gods of the other nations. They said that they understood, and that they would never obey anyone but God.

So Joshua wrote down what they had agreed on, so that they would be sure to remember. He put it all down in a book, and he also put up a special stone under a tree so that it would remind them every time they saw it.

Gideon the Judge

SOON afterwards Joshua died, and was buried in the Promised Land. For the first time the people of Israel were left with no special teacher or leader. At first there were some of the older men who had been friends of Joshua, and as long as they were alive the people listened to God and did what was right. But none of them seem to have known how to pass on to their children the things they knew about God's Plan, so that after a while there was nobody left who knew about it. As they forgot about God, they became muddled and afraid. They began to think there were cross and cruel gods everywhere who might hurt them. They thought there were gods in the woods and the hills and the valleys and in the water. They felt these gods must be kept happy so they built altars and made sacrifices to them. They became bad and cruel.

It was a hard, sad time for them. A wise man called William Penn once said, 'Men must choose to be governed by God, or they will condemn themselves to be ruled by tyrants.' A tyrant is a strong man who wants his own way. When the Israelites listened to as much as they could understand of God, He showed them what to do. When they turned away from Him, they lost everything. The neighbouring fierce tribes came and took them prisoner, and they were very unhappy.

But the great thing about God's Plan is that He never forgets people, even if they forget Him. So although the Israelites were as bad as they could be, God kept His Plan alive by men whom He called judges. One of them was a man called Gideon.

The Israelites had forgotten God for the fourth time since Joshua died, and a tribe called the Midianites had invaded their land, so that they all had to leave their homes and hide in caves. They began to wonder why everything had gone wrong. It made them start thinking about God again, and as they thought they began to see that everything that had happened to them was their own fault. They had stopped doing what they knew was right. They had done things they knew were wrong, and they had nobody to blame but themselves.

At this point God spoke to Gideon and told him he was to save them from the Midianites. At first Gideon found this hard to believe, and he asked God for a sign.

'If you really want to save Israel through me,' he said, 'I will put a sheepskin on the ground and if in the morning there is dew on the sheepskin and not on the ground, I shall know it is true.'

So next day Gideon went to look, and sure enough the fleece was so wet that he was able to wring a bowlful of water from it.

He still could not quite believe that it was God calling him, and he said to God, 'Please don't be angry, but will you do it the other way round now.'

And when the next morning the fleece was dry and the ground was wet, Gideon could not argue any more. He knew that God meant what He said, and that he was the man to take on the freeing of his people.

He called everybody together, and told them they were going to fight the Midianites. God spoke to him again, saying, 'You have collected too many people. If you fight the Midianites with as big an army as that, you will become proud and think you have done it all yourselves. You must talk to the people and tell them that anyone who feels at all afraid can go home.'

Gideon was rather surprised, but he obeyed God, and out of twenty-two thousand men, twelve thousand decided that they were afraid and went home. That left ten thousand.

God spoke again and said, 'You still have too many.' He told Gideon to take the ten thousand to the river to drink, and to pick the men who scooped up the water with their hands, and not those who put their faces into the water and drank as dogs do.

To Gideon's surprise this left him only three hundred men, so when the army had come down from twenty-two thousand to three hundred to fight against thousands of Midianites, it was clear that Gideon could not fight a battle in the ordinary way. He would have to win on the strength of an idea which God gave him.

He divided his three hundred men into three lots of a hundred, and gave each man a trumpet and a lighted lamp inside a stone jar. Then he made his soldiers stand on three sides of the Midianites' camp in the middle of the night. They crept up softly without anyone hearing them. Everyone in the camp was asleep and not expecting anything to happen, which was just what Gideon wanted. When his soldiers had completely surrounded the camp, he gave a signal. The moment his soldiers saw it, they broke the jars which held their lamps so that three hundred lights shone out. At the same time they blew their trumpets, and gave a great shout, 'The sword of the Lord and of Gideon.' It made a terrible noise.

The Midianites woke up suddenly. All they could see were bright lights all round them and a great sound of voices and trumpets. They were quite certain that there was an army of thousands of men coming to kill them, and without waiting to look twice, they all jumped up and ran away as fast as they could. So, because the Israelites were obedient, God gave Gideon the victory. Then the Israelites believed in God again and turned back to Him.

Samuel

AFTER this the Israelites obeyed God for forty years. But in the end they wanted so much to copy all the wrong things which they saw the people around them doing, that they turned away from God again, not once, but many times. You would have thought God would have been very angry. Perhaps if we had been looking after these people we should have been angry and impatient too, and said that we would have no more to do with them.

But God is not like that. He goes on and on caring for people. He knew that it would take a long, long time for men to learn to listen properly, and that this was only the beginning of a story that would take many thousands of years to tell.

Many years after the time of Gideon, when many judges had ruled over the people of Israel, there lived a man called Elkanah and his wife Hannah. Elkanah and Hannah were very fond of each other, but Hannah was unhappy because she had no children. She was so unhappy that one day she went to the temple and prayed earnestly to God to give her a son.

She looked so sad that Eli, the old priest, came up and asked her what was the matter, and she told him. She said too that she had promised God that if He sent her a little boy, she would bring him back to the temple as soon as he was old enough, to learn how to be a priest. She felt that if God gave her a child it would not be hers, but God's, and that she would like to give it back to Him.

Eli said that he felt God was going to answer her prayer; so Hannah went home feeling much happier, and told her husband what had happened.

Sure enough, the following year a boy was born to Hannah and Elkanah. They called him Samuel, which means 'listen to God'. Hannah remembered what she had promised. As soon as Samuel was old enough, she took him to Eli, and left him in the temple to live with the old priest and learn to be a priest too.

At first Samuel understood very little about what he was supposed to do, but he helped Eli in little ways. Every year his mother came to see him, and brought him new clothes to replace the ones which had become too small for him.

One night he was lying asleep when he heard someone call him. He thought that it was Eli, so he ran to ask what he wanted.

'I did not call you,' said Eli. 'Go back to bed again.' Samuel was rather puzzled, but he did as he was told. He lay down and tried to go to sleep, but once more he heard his name called. This time he knew there was no mistake. He went back to Eli and said, 'Here I am, for you did call me.' Again Eli told him to go back to bed.

He had not been there long, when once again he heard the voice call very clearly, and he was so sure it was Eli that he went back once more and said, 'You really did call me that time.'

Then Eli realised that God was trying to tell Samuel something, and he said to him, 'Next time this happens you must sit up and say, "Speak, Lord, for Thy servant heareth."' And that is what Samuel did.

He heard the voice call, and he sat up and said just what Eli had told him, and he listened. As he listened, God told him many things. He showed him how badly the people of Israel were behaving, even Eli's own

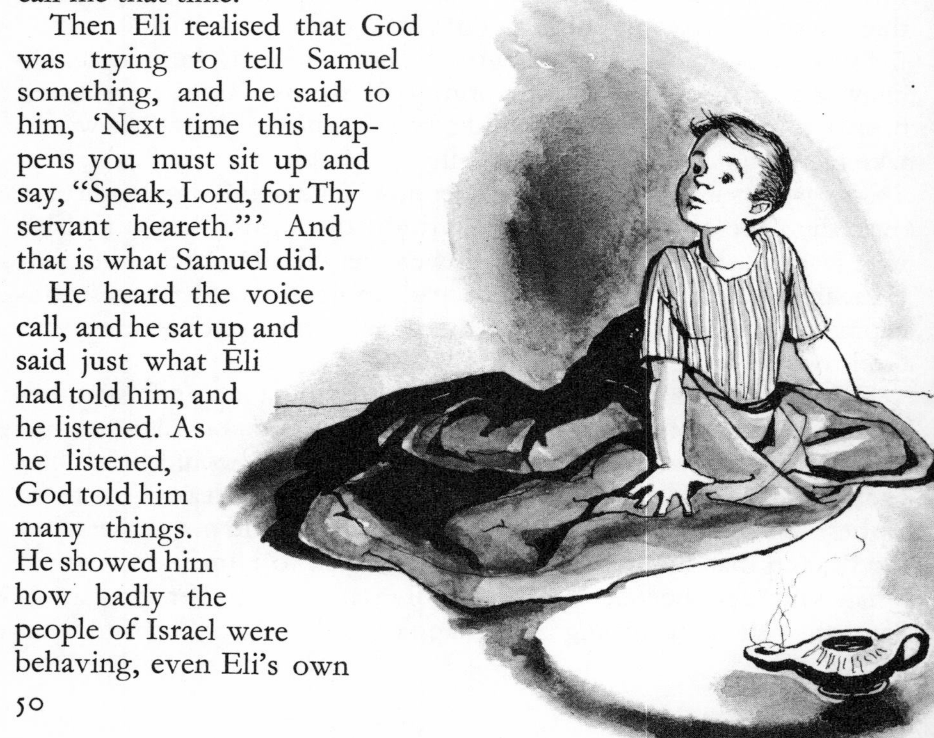

sons, who were priests too, but were not setting a good example. He saw that people were turning away from God, that Eli did not know how to help them and that bad times would come again.

In the morning, Eli asked him what God had said. At first Samuel was afraid to tell him, but in the end he did. Eli was shocked and sorry when he heard it, but he knew in his heart that it was true. He knew that his own sons would not be priests after him, but that Samuel was the one God had called. And that was what happened. Eli died and Samuel became the High Priest, or head priest.

Everyone admired and respected him, but the sad thing was that, like Eli, he did not find the way to help his sons to follow God. It is very important for fathers and mothers to be able to pass on to their children the things they know to be true and right, otherwise so much of God's time is wasted, and His Plan is held up.

When the Israelites saw that Samuel's sons were turning out to be bad men, they said to him, 'Who will lead us when you have gone? Your sons will not, and there is no one else. We must have a king.'

This made Samuel think hard. For hundreds of years the Israelites had had no king but God. They had not always obeyed Him, but He was the unchanging loving spirit to whom they had turned back each time, and Samuel felt that if they started having men to rule them, things would never be quite the same again. He tried to explain this to them.

'How do you know,' he asked, 'that the men whom you choose to rule over you will be good men? They may make slaves of you, and take away your homes and your animals. They may take your sons to be their soldiers, and one day you will find you are sorry you ever thought of having a king, but by then it will be too late.'

However, the people were sure they knew what they wanted. 'All the other nations have kings,' they said. 'We want to be like everyone else and have a king too.'

This was not a good reason for having a king. It is a good thing to have a king when that is part of God's Plan, and the king is someone who helps his people to find that Plan. But kings have not always thought of themselves as men whose chief work was to help their country to find God's Plan. Certainly in those days it was a new idea, and Samuel was not at all sure they would be able to find the right person to take it on.

Saul Looks for the Donkeys

SAMUEL did not know who was meant to be king, but God had already chosen the man He wanted. He was called Saul.

Saul did not belong to one of the important tribes, nor even to an important family in his tribe, which was the tribe of Benjamin. Yet his father was much respected, and Saul himself was a very fine man, tremendously strong and tall and handsome. He had no thought of becoming a king, but lived with his father Kish and helped him with his farming and his animals.

Among the animals were some donkeys. One day these donkeys went astray, so Kish called Saul and said, 'Take one of the servants with you and go and find them.' So Saul and the servant set out together.

They went from one place to another, searching and asking, but the donkeys had completely disappeared. After some days, Saul thought they ought to give up and go home. He said to the servant, 'If we don't get back soon my father will stop worrying about the donkeys and start worrying about us.'

The servant must have believed in God's Plan. He felt they were meant to find the donkeys, but also that they needed help. It happened that by this time he and Saul had come near to the town where Samuel lived, so he said, 'There is a man of God here who knows many things. Perhaps he could show us where to go next.'

Saul was worried at this, for he and his servant had been travelling for several days, and had used up all their food. So Saul said, 'What are we to take him? We can't even take him some bread. What have we got?'

The servant, however, had come prepared. He replied, 'I have a little money with me. We can take that and give it to him.' People in those days reckoned that if a man of God helped them, it was up to them to help him. 'That's a good idea,' said Saul. 'Let's go.'

So they went together towards the town. As they came near to it, they met some young girls coming to the well outside the town to draw water, and they asked them where to find the man of God.

'You've just come at the right moment,' the girls replied. 'This is the day when he goes to make sacrifices on a certain hill. You will just catch him if you go now.'

Saul and his servant followed their direction, and reached Samuel's house as he was leaving. You might have thought that he would be in too much of a hurry to be able to stop and talk to these two strangers who had turned up just as he was setting off for an important sacrifice. Everyone was waiting for him, and nothing could start till he arrived.

However, God had said very clearly to Samuel the day before, 'About this time tomorrow I shall send you a man of the tribe of Benjamin, and I want you to make him king over My people Israel. He will save them from the Philistines, because I feel sorry for My people.' As soon as Samuel saw Saul, he heard God speaking to him again, saying, 'This is the man I was telling you about. He is going to rule over My people.'

Saul, on the other hand, though he saw the old man coming out of the house, did not know that it was Samuel, nor was he quite sure that it was the right house. So he said, 'Please, could you tell me which is the house of the man of God.'

Samuel answered, 'I am the man of God. I am just setting off for the sacrifice. You go on ahead of me. Meet me there, and then come back here to lunch, and I will talk to you later about the things that are on your mind.

'These donkeys, for instance,' he said, 'that you lost three days ago. Don't worry about them, because they are found. Do you know that you are the hope of Israel, you and all your father's family?'

'I?' said Saul, astonished. 'Why, I'm only a Benjaminite, which is the smallest of all the tribes, and my family is least important in the whole tribe of Benjamin. Why do you say such a thing?'

Samuel did not explain any further, but before he left for the hill he called the cook and said, 'You know that shoulder of mutton I told you to set aside yesterday, because we should be needing it? The person for whom I set it aside will be here today.'

So God's Plan also covered what was going to be eaten; and while they were all out at the sacrifice, the servant cooked the meat, and it was ready when they got back.

How Saul Found a Kingdom

GOD seems not only to have told Samuel about the joint, but also to invite a large party, and when Samuel came home with Saul, he introduced him to the thirty other people he had asked.

Then he told the cook to bring in the shoulder of mutton and put it in front of Saul.

'You see,' he said to Saul, 'this is the piece of meat which I have kept specially for you ever since I knew you were coming.'

It was all a great surprise to Saul; but he stayed for the meal, and then he stayed the night.

The next morning Samuel called Saul very early. 'You must soon be on your way,' he said. And he went as far as the end of the town to see Saul off.

As they went, Samuel said, 'Tell your servant to go on ahead. But you stay with me here for a while, so that I may tell you what God wants.' So the servant went on, and did not hear what happened, even though it was mostly due to him that Saul had met Samuel at all. He was a man of God too, and he just did what he was told. No more and no less.

Then, as they stood there, the old priest took some oil and poured it on Saul's head, which is what was done to priests and men chosen by God. It is called anointing. As he did it, Samuel said, 'God anoints you to be the leader of what belongs to Him.'

Then he told Saul that when he reached a certain place he would meet two men who would tell him that the donkeys were found, and that, as Saul had expected, his father was now worrying about him.

'When you have gone a little farther,' said Samuel, 'you will meet three men; one carrying three kids, another carrying three loaves of bread and the third carrying a bottle of wine. They will greet you and give you two of the loaves. After that,' he said, 'you will come to the hill of God where the Philistine soldiers now have their barracks, and there you will meet a group of prophets. They will come towards you singing and playing on different instruments, and will tell you what God wants. At that time the Spirit of God will come to you too, and you will also be able to prophesy.' To prophesy means to pass on God's thoughts to others. Samuel also told Saul that at this moment God would give him a new heart and he would become a new man.

All this happened as Samuel had said. God gave Saul a new heart so that he could hear God's voice and do what He said. Everyone who heard about it was quite surprised. This was not the Saul they had known; and they said to each other, 'Has Saul become a prophet too?'

It made everyone rather curious, and when he got home Saul met one of his uncles, who said to him and his servant, 'Where have you been?' But Saul was not giving anything away yet. He replied, 'We went to find the donkeys, and when we couldn't see them anywhere we went to Samuel.' 'And what did Samuel say to you?' asked his uncle. 'Oh, he just said that the donkeys were found,' said Saul, and left it at that. He said nothing of all that Samuel had told him about being made king. He felt that that had to be done in the right way and at the right time by the right person.

Meanwhile Samuel had called all the people of Israel together. He explained to them all that had happened, how they had wanted a king, and how a king had now been chosen. He asked the tribe of Benjamin to come forward. Out of the tribe of Benjamin he called Saul's family, and they all came forward. He looked down the line, and everyone was there but Saul. Nobody knew where he was, so they asked God what to do. He gave them the thought to go and look in the place where the stores were kept. So they went and looked, and there was Saul hiding.

Poor Saul, he had suddenly found he was afraid of this new responsibility to which God had called him, and he was trying to run away.
They fetched him out and Samuel presented him to the people. He looked very fine standing there, a good head and shoulders taller than anyone else. Samuel said, 'Here is the man whom God has chosen. Do you see how different he is from all of you?'

The people were very pleased, and shouted, 'God save the King.' Samuel wrote down everything that happened in a book and put it in a safe place. Some people gave presents to the new king, and after that Samuel sent the people home.
There were a few men, though, who did not think much of Saul. 'How is this man going to save us?' they grumbled. Perhaps they were jealous because none of them was chosen. So they did not give him any presents, but Saul took no notice of them.

How Saul Did Badly

ALTHOUGH Samuel had picked Saul as God had told him to, he was still not pleased with the Israelites for wanting a king.

He reminded them once more that in the past it had always been God, and no human person, who had come to their rescue when they were in difficulties.

'And now here you are asking for a king,' he said, 'when really God is your King. You've got a king now, but you still need to obey God, because, if you don't, things will go just as wrong as they did before.'

Then he asked God to send rain and thunder to show the people how strong He was, and God did this.

All the people were frightened when they saw it and said, 'Please ask God to forgive us for asking for a king.'

So Samuel reassured them, and said God would certainly never leave His people, and that he, Samuel, would pray for them and show them how to live right.

'Only obey God with all your heart,' he said. 'Think of all He has done for you. But if you still do wrong it will be the end both of you and your king.'

As for Saul himself, he really meant to be a good king. He knew that God had chosen him, and he felt he was God's servant. But quite soon he became more interested in being a king than in doing what God wanted, and it turned out just as Samuel had feared. Things were no longer the same now there was a king.

But there was no turning back. It was a new part of the story.

One of Saul's troubles was that after a year or two he began to think that he knew better than God. He either did a little more or a little less than God told him, and sometimes he did something different altogether.

Also he easily lost his temper. He did not always do what God said, but he was angry if other people did not do what he wanted.

He did silly things too. Once, when he was fighting a battle against the Philistines, he made his soldiers promise that they would not eat anything all day until the Philistines were beaten. Of course by the end of the day the soldiers felt quite weak with hunger, but they did not dare to disobey the king and eat.

In the meantime Saul's son Jonathan had fought another army of Philistines in a different part of the country, and did not know about this order. He beat the ones he was fighting, and when he got back to his father's troops he was hungry too. He and all the soldiers were in a wood, and Jonathan found some honey in a comb. So he dipped his stick into the comb and sucked the end of it just to take the edge off his hunger. It immediately made him feel better, but when his father's soldiers saw this they said, 'Your father made us promise not to eat anything today,' and it made them all feel hungrier than ever.

'Then my father is making it very difficult for people,' replied Jonathan. 'See how much clearer I am now that I have had something to eat. Think how much better you would fight if you had some food'.

However, they thought they had better not, so they went on and fought the next battle in which they beat the Philistines, and captured all their sheep and cattle. By this time they were so hungry that they killed a great many of the animals and ate them straight away.

Moses had laid down certain rules about the way to prepare meat before it was eaten, but the soldiers were far too hungry to bother about them. They simply killed the animals and ate them at once.

Saul was very angry when he heard this, and he made the people come and make a proper sacrifice to show God they were sorry. It never occurred to him that the whole affair was in any way his fault.

However, they had the sacrifice, and then Saul asked God what he should do next about fighting the Philistines.

But Saul's own wants and feelings were already stronger in him than doing what God wanted. So he could not hear God's voice.

He said, 'Someone has behaved badly. We must find out who it is.' That is to say, as soon as he did not see what to do, he thought it was somebody else's fault. He decided to find out who it was, and said that person should be killed, even if it turned out to be Jonathan. He asked whoever it was to own up, but naturally nobody said anything.

Then Saul said, 'We will draw lots to see if it is all of you, or something to do with Jonathan and me.'

'Just as you say,' said the people.

So they drew lots and the draw seemed to show that it was not the people's fault.

'Well, then,' said Saul, 'it lies between me and Jonathan,' and when they drew lots between them (which is a sort of eeny-meeny-miny-mo way of settling things), it seemed to be Jonathan's fault.

His father said to him 'Now tell me what you did.' So poor Jonathan said, 'Well, I only ate a little bit of honey on the end of a stick, and now it seems I have to die for it.'

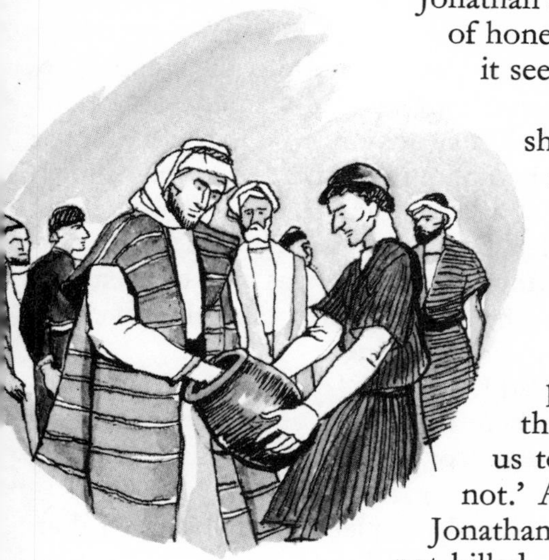

Saul was still determined to show that he was sure he had been right. It was even more important to him to be right than to care for his son or anyone else, and he said, 'Yes, that is so. You must die.'

This was too much for the people. They said, 'What? Jonathan die? Just when he has helped us to win a great victory. Certainly not.' And they rushed up and rescued Jonathan from his father, and he was not killed.

Saul did several other things like this, and soon God called Samuel and told him that He was not pleased with Saul. He had decided to choose another king, and He told Samuel to tell Saul this.

Samuel did not like the thought of telling Saul he was no longer to be king. He was fond of Saul, and he did not want to have to tell him the truth about himself.

So for some time he did nothing about it. Then God called him again, and said that it was no use his being sorry for Saul. He was not doing right, and Samuel was to tell him so. He was also to choose the new king, who was to be one of the sons of a man called Jesse.

David the Shepherd

WHEN Samuel realised that this was what God really wanted, he went to the man called Jesse and said he wanted to make a sacrifice to the Lord, and he and all his sons must be there.

Now Jesse had eight sons. When Samuel asked to see them, they came one at a time, and Samuel looked at each to see if he were the one God had chosen. He looked at the eldest and felt sure it was not him. He looked at the second, and felt sure it was not him either. Then came the third, the fourth, the fifth, the sixth and the seventh, but none seemed to Samuel to be the right one.

When all seven had come, he said to Jesse, 'Are these all the sons you have?' And Jesse replied, 'There is still the youngest, but he is only a boy, and he looks after the sheep.' 'Never mind,' said Samuel, 'bring him here.'

As soon as the youngest boy appeared, Samuel knew in his heart that he was the new king. His name was David, and he was to be the beginning of a new chapter in the story of the people of Israel.

In the meantime Saul was still king. He knew that he had done wrong, and that nothing was going right, and he felt cross and miserable and bad-tempered. He became so bad-tempered that his friends and servants were afraid to go near him. The only thing that helped him to feel better was to listen to music.

One of the men close to the king knew that David played very well on the harp, so they suggested that he should be sent for and play to Saul. Sure enough, the music seemed to help the king. He asked for it often, and became very fond of David, and David too became fond of Saul, and of his son Jonathan.

All this time the armies of Israel were fighting on and off with the Philistines, who lived near by. One day these Philistines suggested that, instead of fighting an ordinary battle with two armies against each other, they should fight in a different way.

They would send out one man, and the Israelites would send out one man. These two men would fight each other. Whoever won, his whole side would have won too, and could take all the others prisoner.

According to the way people did things in those days, it was quite fair. Unfortunately the man the Philistines chose was an enormous giant, called Goliath, and all the Israelites were much too afraid of him for any one of them to go out and tackle him alone.

So Goliath walked up and down calling for someone to go out and fight him, but nobody dared to go.

After some days, David happened to go to the soldiers' camp to see his brothers, who were soldiers. When he heard what was going on, he offered to go and fight the giant himself. He said he knew that God would help him. As soon as King Saul heard this, he offered David his own helmet and coat of mail, but when David tried them, they were much too heavy, so he left them behind. Instead, he picked some round, smooth stones from a stream near by for his favourite weapon, a catapult or sling, and went out to meet Goliath.

As he came near, he put one of the stones into the sling and shot the stone out of it, so that it hit Goliath in the forehead and knocked him over. Then David went up and cut off Goliath's head with the giant's own sword, and the Philistines were so frightened that they all ran away.

Saul's Jealousy of David

THIS was the beginning of much trouble between Saul and David. Everyone began to think what a wonderful young man David was, and to say so. Soon it came to the ears of Saul, who became very jealous.

One day when David was playing his harp to him, Saul threw his spear at him; but David jumped sideways and escaped.

From then onwards all the love Saul had felt for David turned into hate and jealousy. He began to realise that David was going to be the king instead of him, and he thought that if only he could kill him, he could stop that happening.

Saul's son Jonathan was David's greatest friend. They loved each other, and several times when Saul tried to kill David, Jonathan saved his life. They never stopped being friends; and although Saul hated David, David never hated Saul, and always respected him as a king.

Once Saul was hunting David in some mountains, and went into a cave to sleep. While he was asleep, David came in with some soldiers who were on his side. They said to him, 'There is Saul. Why don't you kill him? It would be quite easy.'

But David said, 'No. He is the king. I could never kill the man whom God once called to be a king.'

However, he went up to Saul and cut off a piece of his coat. As he was leaving he called to Saul and woke him up, and told him that he could have killed him. When Saul realised that David had spared his life he was sorry, and said that he loved David. Could not they be friends again? But it did not last. The bad spirit in Saul remained to the end of his life. He could never get over the fact that he had not been successful as a king. In the end both he and Jonathan were killed in a battle, and David became king.

King David

DAVID mourned for Saul and Jonathan. It was a difficult time for him because many of Saul's other friends turned against him. They tried to make another of his sons king over the Northern part of the kingdom, leaving David to be king in the South. But David did become king of the whole country in about 1000 B.C., and everyone accepted him. He conquered some of the countries around, and he captured from a neighbouring chief a town called Jerusalem. He made it into the chief city of his people. He also did much to make the Israelites into a great nation. He made them richer, and other countries started to buy from them and sell to them.

So now they had a capital city, and a stronger army than ever before, an army which won many battles.

David was king for many years, and during that time he did much that was good, but also things that were bad. He was by no means perfect; but one of the best things about him was that he loved God. He knew God loved him, and he loved God in return. He wrote many beautiful songs or psalms about God's goodness, for besides being a king he was a poet.

He remembered the days when he was a shepherd and how he used to look after the sheep, and he often thought of God as a shepherd too, caring for people even if they were sometimes like sheep, and foolish.

One day David was sitting thinking of all that God had done for him and his family, and he began to think of Saul and his family. He wondered what had happened to them, and whether there were any still alive after all the fighting. He discovered that there was an old servant of Saul's called Ziba, so he sent for him and asked if there was anyone left in the family to whom he could show kindness. Ziba replied that Jonathan had had a little boy called Mephibosheth. When Saul and Jonathan were killed, Mephibosheth was five years old, and his nurse picked him up and tried to run away with him to safety, but she was in such a hurry that she fell down. She dropped Mephibosheth, and he was hurt, so that he was never able to walk properly afterwards. 'But,' said Ziba, 'he is still alive. He is grown up and has a son of his own.'

So David had Mephibosheth and his son brought to his house, and he looked after them and gave them back much of the property that had belonged to Saul. He gave them a house of their own, though he also said they could come and have meals with him whenever they liked. For the rest of their lives David looked after Mephibosheth and his son, and Ziba the servant worked for them.

That was one of the good things that David did. He did one specially bad thing too. He had a general in his army called Uriah, and Uriah had a beautiful wife. She was so beautiful that David wished she could be his wife, so he gave orders that next time there was a battle Uriah should be sent to the place where the fighting was hardest so that he would be killed. This actually happened, and when Uriah was dead David took the woman, who was called Bath-sheba, to be his wife.

God was grieved and angry with David over this, and He sent a prophet called Nathan to tell him so. Nathan said that though David and his wife would have a little child, they would not be allowed to keep it, for God would take it away again.

Then David realised how very wrong he had been, and he was sorry and asked God to forgive him, because he knew that he had done something so bad that only God could forgive him. Though God did take the baby, He forgave David, and when David had really changed he wrote a psalm about how his sins had been taken away. This is Psalm 51.

Sin is any bad thought or action which comes between you and God, or between you and another person.

In this psalm David asks God to give him a new heart, and put a right spirit in him. 'Do not cast me away,' he says, 'or take Your holy spirit from me.'

God listened to him, and later on David and his wife had another son called Solomon.

Much the best thing about David was that he never turned to the pretence gods of all the people round about. He never tried to run away from God altogether. Even when he did wrong, he turned back to the Shepherd who looks after all the foolish sheep, to be forgiven and put on the right road again.

This is the Shepherd Song which he wrote. It is the Twenty-third Psalm.

> The Lord is my Shepherd. I shall not want.
> He maketh me to lie down in green pastures: he leadeth me beside the still waters.
> He restoreth my soul: he leadeth me in the paths of righteousness for his name's sake.
> Yea, though I walk through the valley of the shadow of death I will fear no evil,
> For thou art with me. Thy rod and thy staff they comfort me.
> Thou preparest a table before me in the presence of mine enemies.
> Thou anointest my head with oil: my cup runneth over.
> Surely goodness and mercy shall follow me all the days of my life, and
> I will dwell in the house of the Lord for ever.

Before David died God promised that out of his family would come a new king, greater even than David himself, who was to rule over the hearts of the people everywhere in the world.

This was a wonderful promise. It shows how long ago God was thinking and planning ahead, not only for the family of Israel, but for all of us. Hundreds of years were still to go by before the promise came true. Then this Special Person of whom it spoke was born into a family who were the great-great-many-great-grandchildren of King David.

When David died as a very old man, his son Solomon became king.

Solomon

SOLOMON, at the beginning of his reign, about 950 B.C., was a wise and good man. He built a fine temple in Jerusalem to take the place of the Tabernacle or Tent Church which the people had had in the wilderness.

When the Temple was finished, Solomon was praying in it one day, when God asked him what gifts he would like. Instead of asking for money or power or cities, Solomon asked for a wise heart to rule over his people well.

God was pleased with this answer, and said that his prayer would be answered. God also said that if Solomon really wanted to find what was right for himself and the people of Israel, his family after him would rule over them, and the land would be at peace. If, however, he and his family turned aside from the real God to the gods of the nations round about, their greatness would come to an end.

For a while all went well. The fame of Solomon's wisdom spread far and wide, so that kings and queens and great men came from distant lands to talk to him and ask his advice. They often brought gold and silver and valuable gifts, till both the king and the whole country became rich and powerful. Unhappily, the more riches they had, the less they remembered all that God had done for them, and Solomon too became so used to people coming to him for everything, that he grew proud and selfish. The more important money and power seemed to him, the less important did God seem, and Solomon gradually slipped into worshipping the gods of other nations.

God spoke to him again, saying that there was still time for him to change his ways, but that unless he did, many troubles would come upon the nation. However, Solomon had so many wrong ideas by then that he could no longer listen properly to God.

When Solomon turned to the false gods, things went from bad to worse, because these gods were really evil ideas. If people were cruel, they made a statue of a god and said it was a god who liked cruelty. Then they would do all sorts of cruel things and say it was to please the god. A false god is one that you make yourself to suit the way you want to live.

The gods made by the Israelites' neighbours stood for all that was dishonest and unclean, and cruel too, not like the God of the people of Israel, who stands for truth and purity and love.

When King Solomon turned away from what he knew to be right, he lost the sense of God's Plan, and the people lost it too. God had given them everything He had promised them, a country, homes of their own and a king; but they always ended by thinking that what God had given them was more important than God himself.

So just at the moment when they seemed richest and most powerful, they were really in the greatest danger. By the time Solomon died, instead of Israel having become a greater or better country, it was divided and falling apart. Nor had his sons and grandsons learned to live in God's way, and when they came to the throne they made things even worse.

One half of the nation quarrelled with the other half, until there were two countries instead of one, a Northern Kingdom and a Southern Kingdom. The Northern Kingdom kept the name of Israel because it was larger. The Southern Kingdom was just the small state of Judah. The people who lived in Judah were called Judahis, later shortened to Jews. From then on the kings of Israel and the kings of Judah constantly fought against each other in what their people had once called the Promised Land, the land of Canaan.

Israel in Danger

THE little land of Canaan lies along the seashore. In those days the main roads from the neighbouring great countries ran through it. All the great kings of other countries were always wanting to capture the land of Canaan and take it from the Israelites so that they could reach the sea. They wanted to rule over the ports along the coast from which their ships could sail and trade with other lands.

As long as the Israelites were united and were doing what God told them to do, the other nations left them alone. But when they began to quarrel among themselves, the foreign kings saw that the moment they had waited for had come.

When this happened, God sent men called prophets to warn His people. The next story is about a prophet in the Northern Kingdom and a king of that country.

Elijah

ELIJAH was one of the first and greatest of the prophets. The king of Israel at that time, Ahab, was a weak and selfish man with a wicked wife called Jezebel. They not only did wrong themselves, but they got other people to do wrong too.

One day God warned Elijah that a hard time was coming for the country because of the wickedness of the king and queen, who followed false gods. There would be no rain for these years, so that nothing would grow and food would be scarce. God told Elijah to warn King Ahab of this, to give him a chance to change his ways.

But instead the king became very angry with Elijah and wanted to kill him. People often do not like listening to things that are true but uncomfortable. God told Elijah to hide in a cave by a river, where he would be safe from the king, and ravens would be sent to feed him. Elijah did this, and the ravens brought him food every day.

After a time the river dried up, and God sent Elijah to the home of a poor woman who had a little boy. At first the woman found it hard to believe that she could look after Elijah as well as herself and her son, but God promised Elijah that they would have enough food as long as he lived there.

When he had been there a while the little boy fell ill and died, and the woman felt sorry that she had taken Elijah to live with them, because she felt that in some way it was his fault. Elijah realised this, and he prayed, asking God to give the boy back to his mother, because she found his death a hard thing to understand. So the little boy's spirit came back to him, and Elijah picked him up and brought him down from his room and gave him back to his mother.

When the three years without rain had gone by, the king began to get very anxious, and he sent one of his advisers to find Elijah. He felt that Elijah might be able to help, even though he, as king, had fought against all that Elijah was doing to make the country obedient to God's Plan for it.

At the same time Elijah came out of his hiding-place in the woman's house and went to find the king.

As soon as King Ahab saw Elijah, he said, 'Are you the man who has been making all this trouble for Israel?'

And Elijah replied, 'I am not making trouble. The trouble comes from you, since you have followed all these false gods.' Then he went on to say that the time had come for the people to decide whether they were going to follow God or not. So Ahab called the people together, and all the priests of the false god, Baal. Baal was the god of the people who lived in Canaan before the children of Israel came there.

'Suppose,' Elijah said to them, 'we were to try whether your god or my God is the stronger?'

Then he said to the priests of Baal, 'Now put a sacrifice on your altar and see if Baal will send some fire to burn it.' The priests of Baal did this and called upon their god to send fire. They called and prayed all the morning, and all the afternoon. But nothing happened.

Elijah laughed at them and said, 'You must try harder. Perhaps Baal is talking to someone else, or perhaps he's gone on a journey, or he may even be asleep.'

Still nothing happened. There was no one there. Then Elijah called all the people to come close to him, and he repaired God's altar which had been broken down, and made a sacrifice on it. Then, though water was scarce, because of the lack of rain, he made the children of Israel pour water round his sacrifice, so as to make it as hard as possible for any fire to be lit. He made them pour water on it three times. Then he prayed very earnestly to God and asked Him to send fire, so that the people would believe that there really was a God who was stronger than Baal and would turn their hearts to him again. When he had prayed, everybody looked and waited and, as they looked, fire came from heaven, the sacrifice began to burn, and the fire even licked up the water.

At that the people were very much afraid. They realised they had been following their own way and not God's. They fell on their faces and said, 'The Lord, He is God.' The evil priests who had misled the people into worshipping Baal were taken away and killed, and the people made a new start.

God does not always send things that people can see to help them to know that He is there, but He knows what they need at any one time. It may be that the Israelites could not have been turned away from Baal in any other way.

Soon after this, Elijah sent his servant to the top of the nearest hill to look for any sign of rain. The man came back and said that there was nothing in the hot blue sky that he could see.

Elijah told him to go back and look again, but still the servant saw nothing. Elijah sent him back seven times, and at the seventh time the man came running back to say that he could see a little cloud in the distance that looked no bigger than a man's hand.

Elijah knew that this meant that the dry years were coming to an end, and he warned the king to get back quickly to his palace, as it was going to rain very hard. So the king got into his chariot and Elijah ran in front of it all the way, with the rain coming up closer and closer behind.

Elijah and the Still Small Voice

WHEN King Ahab arrived home, he told his wife all that Elijah had done. She was extremely angry, because the prophets of Baal were her friends. She sent a message to Elijah that she would have him killed too before the next day.

So Elijah ran away into the desert. He felt very discouraged, and told God that he did not see much point in going on living. But God looked after him, and encouraged him, and gave him food. Fortunately God does not depend on people's feelings, and He was close to Elijah even though Elijah had lost hope and faith for a time.

He travelled on through the desert until he came to a cave, where he sheltered. God spoke to him and said, 'What are you doing here, Elijah?'

'Oh, God,' Elijah answered, 'I have tried so hard, but the people keep turning away from you. I alone am left, and now they are trying to kill me too.'

This was a gloomy picture, and not quite true. God told him to come out of the cave and watch what would happen.

First there came a great strong wind which even broke the rocks on the mountain; but God was not in the wind.

After the wind there came an earthquake; but God was not in the earthquake.

After the earthquake came a fire; but God was not in the fire.

And after the fire came a still small voice.

Elijah knew that this was God speaking to him. God told him that some of the foreign kings would be allowed to punish the people of Israel if they still refused to do what He said, and that Elijah must take His messages to the king of Israel, and to some of the other kings.

God also told him that there were still seven thousand people in Israel who had refused to follow Baal; so Elijah was not so much alone as he had thought.

After this Elijah had fresh courage. He gave God's messages to the kings, and all the people knew that he stood firmly for what was right, and for making God the real Ruler of the country. This was especially important because of the other tribes who tried to make the Israelites follow their gods.

Later on in the Bible we can read how Elijah is spoken of as a man who played a special part in the unfolding of God's Plan for the whole world.

Towards the end of Elijah's life, God told him that a young man called Elisha was going to carry on his work. Elijah and Elisha worked together for a time.

Before Elijah was taken by God to Heaven, he asked Elisha what gift he should leave with him. Elisha replied, 'Give me a double share of your spirit,' and this was the gift which God gave to Elisha, so that he could always listen for and obey God's messages and help the people to do the same. When Elijah was taken away, Elisha took his cloak and wore it, and this was a sign to the people that Elijah's spirit rested upon him.

Amos and the Plumb Line

ELIJAH and Elisha were followed by a number of prophets between 800 and 700 B.C. who helped the people to understand more and more of what God was like, of His love of what is right, and His care for them.

These prophets said that a nation must have what are called moral standards. 'Moral' means right; 'standard' means something to measure by or follow. So a moral standard is a right way of measuring your life, a right way to follow. The prophets tried to show the Israelites that it was important to live exactly right.

One of them called Amos said that God could always show them what was right. He said God was like a plumb line. Any of you could make a plumb line by tying a weight on to a piece of string. You will find that the string hangs down quite straight. People still use a plumb line to find out if a building is standing straight. They hang it down from the top of the wall or house, and then they can tell if the wall is leaning over or completely upright.

Amos meant by this that God could show people just how

crooked or how straight they were living, and that God's thoughts and ideas could not get through to people who chose to live crooked. This brings us back to God's Plan being people who listen and obey.

Amos was a shepherd. He used to watch his sheep all day long on the top of the hills near Bethlehem, just south of Jerusalem. It was while he was in the fields watching the sheep, thinking about his own country and all the countries round about, that God gave him thoughts, not only for his own people, but for all the neighbouring nations, about what was going to happen to them and about what they could do.

God is always ready to speak to anybody in the middle of their work or at any time, but unless men and women, and children too, are living the best way they know and have hearts open to listen, they do not hear Him.

Although a very large number of the people did not listen to God, there were always some people in Israel who put Him first, because of the bold way in which the prophets spoke out about Him. That is why the prophets were so important. It also meant that there were always some people who had God so much in their hearts that nothing which happened to their country could shake them, and they could tell other people about Him. So more and more people began to see that God's Plan is men and women who listen and obey.

People are sometimes like wireless sets. God is sending messages all the time, but we do not always tune in to hear Him. Of course you cannot turn a switch or press a button in a person, but you can turn your thoughts and your heart in the right direction, and people who think in the right direction more easily go on to live in the right direction. These stories show what happens when people do listen to God and what happens when they do not.

Hosea's Warning and Promise

ABOUT the same time as Amos, there was a prophet called Hosea, who warned the people of the Northern Kingdom that if they continued to disobey God a country called Assyria would attack them and carry their people away. This actually happened. Hosea gave the people this great thought, that God is bound to punish people who deliberately keep on doing what they know to be wrong, instead of turning to Him and asking Him to forgive them and help them to change. But Hosea was the first to tell the people of God's love for them, and of how He longed to welcome them back again if they said they were sorry and truly decided to be different. Hosea helped them to understand God's tenderness towards His children.

Micah and Joel

IN the Southern Kingdom of Judah, about this time, a prophet called Micah spoke bravely to the king and the people, telling them that even if they were rich and powerful, that was not enough, and would not please God. Nor could they excuse themselves for being cruel and greedy and selfish by sacrificing sheep and rams to God. God did not want these. What He asks for is something different. 'He has shown you, O man, what is good. What He asks of you is to do justly, and to love mercy and to walk humbly with your God.'

Micah spoke of a day that would come when all the nations would turn to God. 'God will teach us,' he said, 'His ways, and we will walk in His paths. He will judge between the nations, and will reprove the strongest nations. And they will turn their swords into ploughs, and their spears into pruning hooks, and they will not learn war any more.'

He was also the prophet who foretold, seven hundred years before it happened, that a King, who would save His people, was to come out of Bethlehem.

There was another prophet called Joel, who lived in Judah just after Elijah's time. In his day everybody was saying that 'the Day of the Lord would come', when everything would become right for the Jews again. But just at that point God let a whole cloud of locusts come and eat up everything in Judah, and Joel told the people that this was what the 'Day of the Lord' would be like for them all if they did not change their hearts and listen to God.

He said that they must turn to God with all their hearts, and then God would take them back again and make everything different. He said that one day this would certainly come true and then something tremendous would happen to everybody in the world. The exact words in the Bible are in *Joel*, Chapter 2, verses 28–29. This means that everybody, boys and girls, young and old, will be able to listen to God and each one be told what they are expected to do, and that every one of them will then have a full share in making the new kind of world that everybody wants to see.

Habakkuk

ANOTHER prophet was called Habakkuk. He talked about writing down what God said. He climbed a tower, and sat there quietly waiting. He was told by God to write down the vision that came to him, and to make it so clear that anyone going by could read it. And even if it seemed to take time before God's promises were fulfilled, said Habakkuk, they would certainly come true if people obeyed. He said, 'The just will live by his faith.'

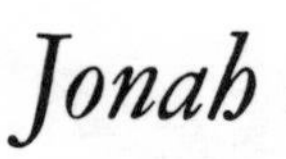

Jonah

JONAH was an Israelite who was afraid of the great country Assyria, which was to attack and carry away the Northern Kingdom of Israel. Assyria's biggest city was Nineveh, and explorers have found remains of it. God told Jonah to go to Nineveh and give the people there the chance to change. The best way to treat enemies is to plan how to help them to change. Then they can become friends.

But Jonah hated and feared Nineveh, so he took a ship going in the opposite direction. The rest of the story in *Jonah* tells of the storm and of the whale which swallowed Jonah and took him back to shore, and how he changed and went to Nineveh after all, and very many people there decided to live differently.

The Northern Kingdom Comes to an End

DURING the time of the prophets there were both good and bad kings. The trouble was that the good kings were not wholly good, for though they themselves wanted to do the right things, they were half-hearted about getting rid of what was wrong. So the whole country became rather half-hearted too. The people who still had the right ideas had no fight in them, so after a while there was no fight left in the country either. This is called compromise, and when people compromise they always get into trouble.

You remember that the country had been divided into two parts many years before. One day a powerful king from Assyria swooped down on the Northern part of the Israelites' land, and took the people prisoner. He carried them all away, and from then on they were never heard of again. In their place he sent all sorts of foreigners from other conquered countries to live in the Northern Kingdom in 721 B.C., and from then on this part was called Samaria, and the people who came to live there were called Samaritans. They were despised by the Jews who stayed in the Southern Kingdom of Judah. The Jews always pointed out that they were the only real Israelites left, and they hated these new people who had come in and taken over the Northern country.

So now this family of people, for whom God had cared so much, had shrunk to a small handful, very much alone. There were enemies all round them, who were just waiting for a chance to come and capture the few who were left. But this was not to happen yet.

Isaiah

IN the Southern Kingdom one of the great prophets was called Isaiah. One day God spoke to him and said, 'Although these are my children and I have cared for them and looked after them all these years, they still do not do what I say.'

Then He said, 'Oh, you evil children. You kill animals as sacrifices but it does not mean anything any more. Why do you not wash away all your wrong ways? However bad you are, you could become clean and white like snow. If that happened, everyone would come running to you to find out how to live. If it does not happen, everything will go wrong.

'I planted something in your hearts that was meant to be very wonderful. It was meant to be like a vineyard full of beautiful grapes; but now it is all weeds, and the grapes are not beautiful fruit, but small, like wild ones.'

He said more too. He said, 'You are greedy. You just try and get more and more for yourselves. All the things you want to do are wrong, so that you say wrong things are right. You have become proud and think you know best, and many of you drink too much wine. If this goes on, strong nations will come and conquer you. They will see how weak and selfish and greedy you have become, and you will be beaten.'

When Isaiah heard this, he said to God, 'But I am just as bad. I am a bad man in a bad nation. I cannot even say things that are clean and true.'

It seemed to him that an angel came and touched his mouth with a hot coal, and told him that the sin in him was burnt up and taken away and he was forgiven. Then he heard the voice of God saying, 'Whom shall I send?' and Isaiah found himself answering, 'Here am I. Send me.'

God told him to go to the people of Judah and warn them of what would happen if they did not change, and give them a chance to do better.

King Hezekiah of Judah

THE king of Judah of this time, between 700 and 600 B.C., was called Hezekiah. He decided that the country must stop being half-hearted and putting up with wrong gods and bad priests who made people do wrong things.

His father had made sacrifices to all the false gods, and the Temple had become very dirty and neglected. In the very first month that he was king, Hezekiah called all the priests together and said to them, 'God is angry with us because of the way we have behaved, and I feel it is time we did something to show that we are really sorry.' He suggested that they might start by getting the Temple clean.

The priests agreed, and they went to work, clearing out first of all the rubbish from it, and then all the dirt. King Ahaz, Hezekiah's father, had broken all the beautiful cups and bowls belonging to the Temple, and simply left them lying about, and the place had not been cleaned for years. The priests were determined to get everything right, and they worked so hard that in sixteen days it was all finished.

When it was done, Hezekiah got up early in the morning and called all the rulers of the city to the Temple to offer sacrifices. But this time the sacrifices were to show that they were sorry, and all the people from the city came too.

They were all so glad that it had happened, and so quickly, because God had been at work in their hearts.

Hezekiah then sent letters all over the country to ask everyone to come to Jerusalem for the Passover. The Passover was the time when the people of Israel remembered the night when God had brought them out of Egypt; but it was many years since anyone had kept it properly, and some had not remembered it at all.

Many people just laughed when they got the message and would not come. But others came, and the king told them that he needed their help in getting rid of all the wrong things in the country. To start with, he would like them to pull down the altars of the idols that were in Jerusalem. They promised to help and went off and pulled them down. Then they came back for the Passover Feast.

Many people had forgotten how this feast should be kept, but Hezekiah prayed, and asked God to forgive them all for any mistakes they might make in celebrating it. So He healed their hearts, and they all said where they had done wrong and that they were sorry.

There was great joy in the country. There had not been so much joy in Jerusalem since the days of King David. For the first time for many years all the people had started doing what God wanted and putting wrong things right. The king had led the way, and the people sang songs of praise in the Temple.

When the festival was over, they all went out to the country around and pulled down the rest of the altars to the false gods, and they fought against the spirit of disobedience which had gripped the nation, so that it became God's once more.

Isaiah and Hezekiah

HEZEKIAH'S little kingdom was very much alone now that the Northern Kingdom had been conquered, and its people taken prisoner. It did not look strong or powerful, and the King of Assyria, who had taken the Northern Kingdom, thought he could now take this land too. In fact, he did succeed in taking several of the walled cities. He even made King Hezekiah give him some of his treasures.

This Assyrian king's name was Sennacherib. After he had taken the cities he marched to Jerusalem and camped round the walls. The captain of the army sent messengers up to the walls to try and frighten the Jews into giving the city to the Assyrians. One of them, an officer called the Rabshakeh, spoke to all the people who were standing along the wall looking at this great army which had come against them.

'Do not let your king tell you that God will help you,' said the Rabshakeh. 'It is not true. We are going to win. It would be better to give in now. After all, we have beaten all the other peoples who thought that their gods would save them. They could not. Why should you think your God can save you?'

The people felt sure that the God they knew was quite different from all the other people's gods. So they backed up King Hezekiah when he sent word to them telling them not to answer the Assyrians. They let the Rabshakeh go on talking without paying any attention.

All the same, King Hezekiah was worried, and he sent for Isaiah to ask him to pray for the country. He knew what the prophet had said would happen to his people. It had already happened in the Northern Kingdom, and he was afraid that it might happen to his country too, in spite of all the things he had put right. But Isaiah sent back a message telling him not to be afraid, because Sennacherib would go away without hurting them. This is exactly what happened. News came of trouble in Sennacherib's kingdom, and he had to go home.

A little later Sennacherib came again with an army. Hezekiah prayed about this threat too, and went to Isaiah.

Isaiah again replied that the Assyrian king would not take the city.

He said that God had told him that He had a plan for His people, and that, though in the end they would be taken prisoner, the time was not yet. And there would always be a few people out of whom God's Plan would grow and continue.

It happened as Isaiah had said. Many of the men in the Assyrian army died of plague in the night. One writer who lived in those days tells a story of how some mice came and ate all the Assyrians' bow-

strings. So for one reason and another they could not attack Jerusalem, and those who were still alive went back to their own country.

Hezekiah was rather pleased with himself after this. He thought that he and his armies, instead of God, had got rid of Sennacherib.

Then Hezekiah was taken ill. Isaiah came and told him that he had got proud. Hezekiah realised that it was true. He told God that he was sorry, and soon afterwards he began to get better.

He lived for some years longer, but towards the end of his life he did something about which he did not consult Isaiah, and which Isaiah felt was wrong. Some men from a rich and powerful city called Babylon came to see him. They were the enemies of the Assyrians. They brought Hezekiah presents, and seemed very anxious to know if he were feeling better. Because they seemed so kind, and because they might help against Assyria, Hezekiah took them all over his palace, and showed them everything he had, and all his treasures. Then the men from Babylon returned home.

When Isaiah heard of this he was sorry, and felt that the king had been unwise. He said it was no good trusting in other men to keep off Assyria. Only God would do it. Besides, he said, the visitors were not true friends, but greedy people who only wanted to find out what Hezekiah had, so that one day they could come and take it.

'And that,' said Isaiah, 'is what will happen. In days to come, your people will be taken away to Babylon and the treasures with them.'

But because Hezekiah had united his country, it was still strong, and what Isaiah had said did not come true during Hezekiah's lifetime.

Isaiah's Special Message

ISAIAH was a man who saw things clearly. He was honest about himself and his nation, and so he could see much more clearly than most people what God wanted.

Besides all that God told him about his own time, He also began to tell him of something that would happen many years later. Isaiah was the first man who understood that God's Plan was one particular Person. The reason he felt so sure that the Assyrians were not going to destroy all the people of Judah was because God had told him that this Person would be born into His chosen family.

He said that a child would be born, a child who would be called Wonderful, Counsellor, the Mighty God, the Prince of Peace, and that one day the whole world would be ruled by Him.

God also said that a little root had been planted in the family of Jesse which would grow into something which everyone would want. (Jesse was David's father, so this meant that the Person would be born into the family of David.)

God talked of Him as a King who would be full of goodness, and would help other kings to rule well, and later on He said the world would become quite a different place because of Him.

'Even the desert will be glad, and blind men will see, and lame men will even be able to jump,' said God. 'It will be like a good road for people to walk along. They will find joy and gladness, and sorrow and sighing will flee away.'

He spoke too of someone who would come first to prepare the way, to make ready the road.

Later on, when things went badly wrong for the people of Israel, they felt that their only hope lay in this King who would come one day and save them, and rule over the whole world. They thought that probably, as this King was going to be so great, they would become great again, and be a powerful nation. They did not see that God was showing them that His Plan might begin with them, but that it would spread out to the world, for it is a gift to the whole world.

There was something else in the book of Isaiah to which they did not pay so much attention.

It was that this King would also be a servant, a servant of God; that in many ways He would have a sad life. He would be a Man of Sorrows, who knew sadness.

Like the lambs that were killed in sacrifices, this Man would be sacrificed because of the wrong things that people do. He would feel all the sadness of everyone's sins, and carry the load of it Himself.

Isaiah understood the purity and the Holiness of God, and the need to let Him wash away our sins, just as we wash away the dirt from our bodies. He wrote 'Come now, let us talk together,' said the Lord. 'Though your sins be as scarlet they shall be as white as snow, though they be red like crimson, they shall be washed away as wool is washed.'

Isaiah did not understand all this, but he knew that the things God said were true, so he wrote them for everyone to read and remember, and that is how we know about them today.

The sayings that men like Isaiah had from God and wrote down are called prophecies, and at the end of this book of Isaiah there is a wonderful picture in words of the new world, with a great light shining in people's hearts. It says that wherever people see that light shining in whatever person, in whatever country, men will come flocking to it.

'Nations will come running to you,' he says, 'because of the Lord your God.'

* * *

Here are some words by another prophet who wrote about this time. No one knows quite who wrote them, but they are to be found in *Isaiah*, Chapter 40. He writes of the wonder and greatness of God, 'who has measured the waters of the world in the hollow of His Hand, and measured out the Heavens'. To Him, he says, the nations are like a drop in a bucket, they are counted as the small dust in the scales, and He takes up the isles as a very little thing. The writer shows that the idea of God as a loving Father was beginning to grow in men's hearts. There are some lovely lines where it says, 'Comfort ye, comfort ye my people. Speak to Jerusalem tenderly.' Then the writer says that God will feed His flock like a shepherd, and gather the lambs into His arm; that He will give power to people who are discouraged, and strength to people who feel weak; and he ends with the words, 'They that wait upon the Lord shall renew their strength; they shall mount up with wings as eagles; they shall run and not be weary, and they shall walk and not faint.'

Josiah to Zedekiah

AFTER Hezekiah there were several bad kings of Judah, and then one more good one called Josiah, about 650 B.C.

Josiah became king when he was only eight years old, and when he grew up, he and the High Priest, Hilkiah, tried to clean up the country completely. They set about repairing the Temple, which had again begun to fall into ruins. While doing this, Hilkiah found a book of laws and customs that had been hidden away for many years. Hilkiah sent it to the king, who had it read aloud to him by his secretary or scribe. It turned out to be a book containing all that Moses had told his people about how to obey God.

When it was read to King Josiah, he saw how far the people of Judah had gone from the way of living that Moses had taught. He was troubled, and asked a prophetess called Huldah for her advice.

She replied that because of the way the people had lived great misfortunes were going to fall upon the land, but that as Josiah had really fought for the right things, God would take him to Himself before the bad times came. This came true. When Josiah was still a young man, the king of Egypt moved to attack the neighbouring kingdom of Assyria. Josiah's little kingdom lay between Egypt and Assyria, and he decided to try and stop the Egyptian king, Pharaoh

Necho, from crossing his land. Necho warned him not to, saying, 'I'm not fighting against you, but against the Assyrians, and you had better keep out of the way, or you will be killed.'

Josiah would have been wiser to listen to him, for, as Necho said, 'My words came from God.' But he was pig-headed. He disguised himself, hoping to pass unnoticed, and joined in the battle.

His disguise was in vain, for the Egyptian archers shot at him and hit him, and he said to his servants, 'Take me away, for I am badly hurt.' So they took him off the battlefield, placed him in the spare chariot which they had, and brought him back to Jerusalem to be looked after. But when he got there he died.

There was great sadness among all the people of Judah when they heard of his death. They would have been sadder still if they had known that it was the beginning of the end, for Josiah was the last good king of Judah.

After his death, nothing really went right again. The people of Judah did what they wanted rather than what God said. It was not that they did not know any better, but that they turned away from what they knew was right. This made them weaker than the other nations, who believed very much in the only way of living they knew, even though it was a bad one. The people of Judah wobbled between good and bad without deciding on either.

The next king was Josiah's son, Jehoahaz, but after three months Necho, king of Egypt, came and took him prisoner, and made his brother Jehoiakim king instead. Jehoiakim lived such an evil life that he set no example to his people and soon Nebuchadnezzar, king of Babylon, captured Jerusalem and took Jehoiakim back there as a prisoner. His eight-year old son was made king instead, but the poor child did not make a good one either, which is not very surprising.

Three months later Nebuchadnezzar took the boy king to Babylon too, leaving his uncle Zedekiah to rule Judah. Zedekiah had the chance of being a good king, for the prophet Jeremiah, who had been the friend and adviser of his father Josiah, was there to help him. Jeremiah had also tried without much success to advise Zedekiah's brother Jehoiakim. Unfortunately Zedekiah was a weak man, and would not pay any attention either, until it was too late.

Jeremiah and Ezekiel

JEREMIAH was the son of a priest, but he did not expect to become a prophet. So he was surprised and afraid when one day, while King Josiah was still alive, God spoke to him and said, 'I have called you to be a prophet to the nations.'

'Oh, Lord,' he said, 'I cannot speak. I am a child.'

But God answered, 'Don't say "I am a child". For you shall go wherever I send you and say whatever I tell you. Don't be afraid of people's faces, for I am the Lord your God and I shall be with you.'

Jeremiah was to need all the courage God could give him in the years that followed. He told the king and the people all that would happen to them unless they changed their ways, but hardly anyone believed him. God told him of enemies coming from every side, and warned him not to marry, because there was going to be no chance of bringing up a family in the days that were coming.

One day God told Jeremiah to go and watch the potter at work, for He had something to teach him. Jeremiah went, and found that the potter had just made a jar, but it had not turned out as he had hoped. The clay was still wet, so he squashed it into a lump and started again. This time the jar was as the potter had meant it to be. God showed

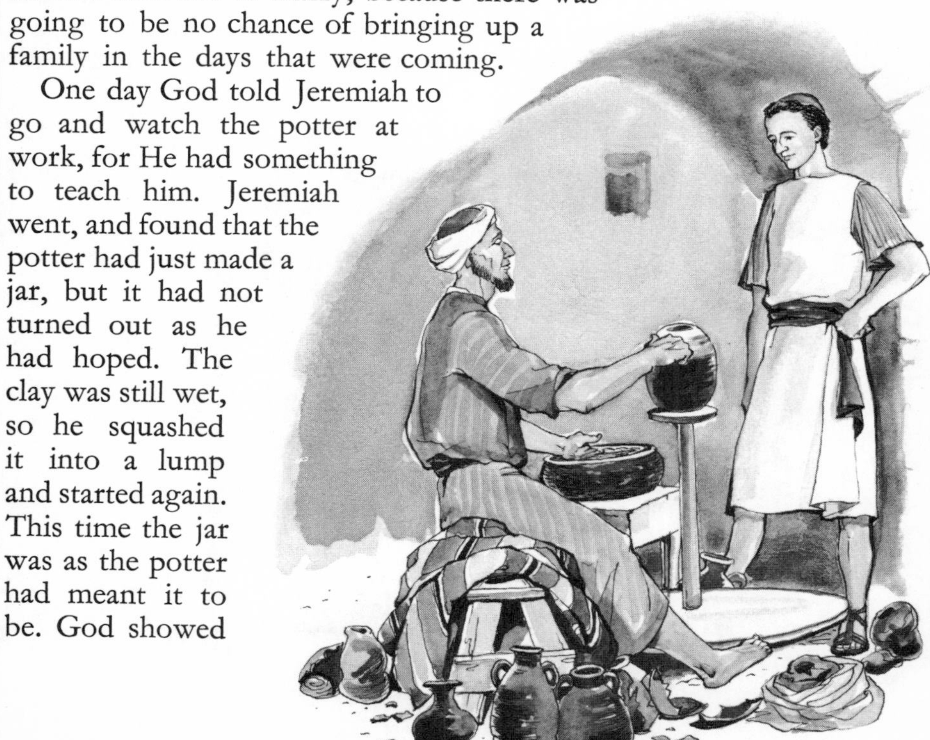

Jeremiah through this that if people did not turn out right, they too would have to be destroyed before they could be remade, and this was the message that Jeremiah must take to the people of Judah.

He went back and told them that they would be broken like a potter's jar if they did not listen to what God was saying to them. But the only result was that he was put in the stocks.

He found all this hard to bear. He was an ordinary person, just like you and me, and, like us, he hated to be laughed at. He argued quite a lot with God, saying, 'Oh, God, why do you let this happen to me? I have done what you said, but everybody makes fun of me.'

However, there was something in his heart which made him go on in spite of all the difficulties.

Once he was put in prison by King Jehoiakim, but he sent for the king's secretary, Baruch, and dictated a message to Jehoiakim warning him of what was going to happen. Baruch wrote out Jeremiah's message and took it to the king. It was winter, and a fire was burning in the room where Baruch read the message. It made Jehoiakim so angry that he seized it, cut it up with his penknife and threw it into the fire. But burning it did not stop the warning coming true, nor did it stop Jeremiah from having it written out again.

By now he was known as a man of God. Once Zedekiah, who had now become king, sent him a message asking whether the Jews would defeat the king of Babylon, who was just about to make war on

them. God's message to the king, through Jeremiah, was that he and all his people would be taken to Babylon as prisoners, and never come back.

The message also said, 'Tell the king that no one will mourn for him as they did for his father, Josiah.'

Again nobody believed Jeremiah. They said everything would turn out all right in the end, and some even suggested that Jeremiah should be killed, but others would not agree to this.

Jeremiah was not afraid. He told them all that it was no good going on blindly hoping for the best, and living wicked lives. They would be captured, and they would be wiser to accept it as part of God's Plan for them.

Jeremiah told them that in the land to which they would be taken they would be able to marry and have children, and settle down. 'And,' he said, 'you must pray for the peace of the city where you will be, and at the end of seventy years your descendants will be able to come home again.'

Then God said how much He loved them, in spite of all their wrong doings. He said, 'I have loved you with an everlasting love,' and He told Jeremiah to tell them that if they would learn the lessons He wanted to teach them through their captivity, they would come back to Jerusalem with something new for the whole world.

They would return, not to get power for themselves, but to bring God's Plan to all the nations, so that Jerusalem might become like a broadcasting station for God's words to go to the world. This would prepare the way for a Saviour whom He would send there.

When that time came, He said, no one would be able to say that 'the fathers have eaten sour grapes, so the children's teeth are set on edge', which is another way of saying that when anything goes wrong with you it is someone else's fault. Everyone was going to be responsible for his own wrongdoing.

This would fulfil another of God's great promises to men, which was that 'I will put My law in their inward parts and write it in their hearts, and I will be their God, and they shall be My people.'

God said that people would not need to go round any more saying, 'Know the Lord'; for everyone would know Him, from the least to the greatest.

He also said, 'I will forgive them for what they have done wrong, and not remember it any more.'

But it may be that the time had gone by when one man could make a whole nation listen. They would have to learn some other way.

The Warnings Come True

THE people of Judah listened neither to the warnings of the prophet nor to his promises, but he went on faithfully telling them what was going to happen to them until they were tired of hearing him. They said he was siding with the enemy, and he was put in a dungeon, which is an underground prison.

By this time the Babylonians were besieging the city, so you would have thought that the people would have begun to think that things were not going too well. The king himself at last began to realise this. He sent for Jeremiah secretly and asked, 'Is there any word from the Lord?'

But the word from the Lord remained the same as it had been for many years, that the king and all the people were going to be taken prisoner. Jeremiah repeated this and asked one thing for himself, which was not to be put back in the dungeon. The king, who was perhaps beginning to wonder whether he had really been fair to Jeremiah, gave orders that he should be put in the courtyard of the prison, and be well treated.

However, certain men went to King Zedekiah and said, 'This man is discouraging everyone by saying we are going to be defeated by the Babylonians. He ought to be killed.'

Zedekiah was too weak to stand up for Jeremiah, and he let him be taken and put in a deep pit filled with mud, where Jeremiah would certainly have died but for a man called Ebed-melech, from Ethiopia.

Ebed-melech went to the king and told him that the prophet would starve to death if he was left where he was. So the weak and wobbly king changed his mind again, and said, 'You may get him out.'

Then Ebed-melech took a gang of men and a rope and some old rags. He went to the pit and threw the rags down to Jeremiah, telling him to put them under his arms, so that the rope would not rub him. Then Ebed-melech let down the rope and pulled him up.

By this time the king was really frightened. The Babylonians were

all round the city. He sent for Jeremiah again and asked him what was going to happen.

'Are you sure you won't kill me if I tell you?' asked Jeremiah.

'I promise not to,' answered the king.

Jeremiah told him that he would be wiser to surrender. If he gave himself up now, he would not be killed, but if he tried to escape he would be.

'But I shall be laughed at if I surrender,' said poor, weak Zedekiah.

'If you will only obey God, you will be all right,' replied Jeremiah. 'I beg you to obey Him.'

Zedekiah did not know which way to turn. He was afraid of God, but more afraid of his nobles.

'Don't tell my princes about our talk,' he begged. 'Tell them that you were just begging me not to send you back to the same prison.'

Jeremiah agreed, and they accepted his story.

Soon after this, Jerusalem was taken by the king of Babylon. Zedekiah, in spite of Jeremiah's warning, tried to escape, and was captured, as Jeremiah had foretold. His eyes were put out and he was taken in chains to Babylon.

Jeremiah, on the other hand, was set free by the conquerors and allowed to go about among the people, and although they had not listened to him in the past, they turned to him, hoping that now he would tell them something they wanted to hear.

But Jeremiah never tried to please anyone. He told them what God told him, which was that they should stay where they were and obey God. If they tried to run away, they would all be killed.

However, most of them had already made up their minds to escape to Egypt, and they hoped Jeremiah was going to tell them that that was what God wanted them to do. When they heard him say they were to stay, they were furious.

They said, 'You are lying. God has not told you to tell us not to go to Egypt.'

They gathered up their families and their friends and went to Egypt. They took the brave old prophet with them, and neither he nor they were ever heard of again, though there are records of some of the last things he said to the obstinate, disobedient people after they had reached Egypt.

It was his last call to them to turn back to God, and a final warning that they could not escape Him by running away.

In the meantime Nebuchadnezzar had taken the kings of Judah and many of the leaders away to Babylon. Only a few poor farmers and peasants were left. Among those who were carried off was a young man called Ezekiel. He took on the care of the prisoners in Babylon, as Jeremiah had tried to do with those left behind in Jerusalem. They both said that every single person would have to be responsible for listening to God and obeying, and so have their share in making the future good or bad.

Both Jeremiah and Ezekiel, like Isaiah, saw that even if the Jews' country was occupied and its people scattered those people could take God's message all over the world, provided His laws were written in their hearts and obeyed.

Over the years a small number of men and women had kept God in their hearts, and so when they were taken off to Babylon, they did not forget Him, nor fall into the bad ways of the people of Babylon. They took with them a faith stronger than the Babylonians had.

Ezekiel helped them. He put his message in pictures. He said that people without God were like dry bones lying in a valley, but when God's spirit breathed on them they became living people again, made of flesh and blood. God promised to give everyone a new heart and a new spirit so that all men would know that He could rebuild ruins and replant deserts—that He could make new nations out of new people.

The Fiery Furnace

AFTER Ezekiel had been in Babylon for some years Nebuchadnezzar took Jerusalem again. Among his prisoners this time was a boy named Daniel, with his three friends Shadrach, Meshak and Abednego.

There are many stories about the people of Jerusalem who were carried off to Babylon, and among the best known ones are those of Daniel and his friends. These young men were among those whom God had called to carry His Plan into what is known as the Exile.

Nebuchadnezzar gave orders that Daniel, Shadrach, Meshak and Abednego should be brought up with the Babylonian princes. Living in the king's palace they soon realised that it was going to be hard to stick to what they had been taught at home. The Babylonian princes with whom they were now living were given a lot of very good food, and Daniel was afraid that he and his friends might come to be more interested in the food than in doing God's will. So he and they asked the man in charge of them if they could have much plainer food. At first this man was afraid to do what they asked, in case they should get thin and ill, and the king would be cross, especially as he had said the Jews were to be treated exactly like the Babylonians. But he tried it, and found that Daniel and his friends did just as well on the plainer food, which was a sort of porridge, so he went on giving it to them, and they grew stronger through learning not to be greedy.

As they learned to say 'no' to themselves, they also learned to say 'yes' to God. He helped them to be wise and honest, so that as they grew up, the king trusted them more and more.

Many years before, Joseph had also been the trusted friend of the king of Egypt, for the same reason. Like Joseph, these four friends became the men whom the king trusted most. Shadrach, Meshach and Abednego were put in charge of one of the country districts, and Daniel stayed in Babylon with the king.

This did not please the Babylonian princes. They thought that they should have been put in charge, and not the men who had been prisoners. So they waited for a chance to turn the king against them.

It soon came. Nebuchadnezzar gave orders for a big golden statue to be made and put up in the part of the country where Shadrach, Meshach and Abednego were in charge. Then he said that on a certain signal everyone was to kneel down and pray to it. Anyone who disobeyed would be thrown into a fiery furnace. The statue was made, the signal was given, and everyone knelt down and prayed to the statue. Everyone, that is to say, but three. These three were of course Shadrach, Meshach and Abednego, who were determined not to do anything which dishonoured God. But various people saw them refuse to kneel, and went running to tell the king.

Although Nebuchadnezzar trusted these three men completely, and knew how much they helped him, he was angry at their not doing exactly what he said. So he gave orders for them to be taken immediately and thrown into the furnace.

He had it made specially hot, so that they should be burnt up at once. But when they were thrown in, they were not hurt at all. The king could see them walking about in the fire, and he could also see a fourth man with them who looked, he said, like a Son of God.

The king spoke to them, calling them the servants of the most High God, and asked them to come out. Out they came, without even the smell of fire on them. Nebuchadnezzar said, 'Blessed be the God of Shadrach, Meshach and Abednego,' and he made a law that from then on nobody was to worship any God but theirs.

The three friends went back to the district which they had governed before, and Daniel stayed on with the king as his adviser.

Daniel continued for fifty years as counsellor to the kings after Nebuchadnezzar. He kept telling them that if they did not change as Nebuchadnezzar had done, Babylon would be taken from them, and when he was about sixty-five, it happened. One night at that time, the king, whose name was Belshazzar, gave a great feast, and in the middle of the feast a hand appeared writing four words on a wall. Daniel told Belshazzar that the writing meant that he and Babylon had been weighed in the scales and found wanting. Because of this Babylon would be given to the Medes and Persians. Sure enough, that very night Cyrus, the King of the Medes and Persians, sent his general, who captured the city of Babylon and killed many of the people, including Belshazzar.

Daniel in the Lions' Den

THE Medes and the Persians over whom Cyrus ruled lived in two countries on the other side of the high mountains east of Babylon. Cyrus and his son and grandson trusted Daniel as the kings of Babylon had done. They took him to the capital Susa, also called Shushan, and there Cyrus' grandson Darius made Daniel his chief counsellor. He saw that Daniel was not on any man's side, but on God's side; and that he stood not for who was right, but for what was right. It made him fearless in telling anybody what God had told him ought to be done.

Darius consulted Daniel about everything, until the princes of the Medes and Persians became so jealous that they started thinking of how to get rid of Daniel, who must have been quite an old man by then, of over seventy.

They looked in the book of laws to see if Daniel was breaking any of them. But he was not. Everybody liked him, and Darius would not hear anything against him. So the princes thought of a trick that would force Darius to punish Daniel.

Darius, although he valued Daniel, must have been rather a vain man. He liked hearing nice things about himself, and he liked everyone to think that he was wonderful. His vanity gave the princes their chance. They went to Darius and suggested that he should give an order that for thirty days nobody should pray to any other man or other god but himself. If anyone did so, he would be thrown into a den of lions.

Sad to say, Darius agreed to this. When he had approved the order, the princes said, 'Remember that by the laws of our country, the country of the Medes and Persians, once the king's order has been given it can never be altered.'

Darius said he would remember, without stopping to think what a wrong and foolish idea this was, and where it might lead.

Very soon the order came to the ears of Daniel, and all the princes watched to see what he would do. He could, of course, have gone quietly into a corner where nobody could see him and prayed. But he knew exactly why the order had been given, and he felt it was a chance for him to trust God, and to show that he trusted Him.

So he opened his window and knelt there in front of all the people and prayed to God three times a day.

The princes, who had been hoping that this would happen, went quickly to Darius and said, 'O King, live for ever' (which is what people said to kings in those days), 'that man Daniel, who was a prisoner, is paying no attention to your order, but is praying three times a day to his own God.'

Then Darius saw too late what he had been led into doing, and he tried in every way to put it right and save Daniel. He argued with the princes all day, right until the sun went down, but all they would say was, 'It is the law of the Medes and Persians. What the king says cannot be altered.' In the end Darius gave in. He may even have thought that if he did not do as the princes said, they might throw him to the lions too. Anyway, when night came he sadly gave the order for Daniel to be taken and put in the den. But he said to Daniel, 'Your God, whom you serve continually, will deliver you.'

The king had a stone rolled against the door, and he sealed it with his signet ring. Then they all went away.

The king was very unhappy, for he knew he had done wrong. He would not eat anything, and when he went to bed he could not sleep. Early in the morning, after tossing and turning all night, he hurried down to the den and called to Daniel. Hardly daring to hope that he could still be alive, he said, 'Daniel, was your God, whom you serve continually, able to deliver you from the lions?'

To his great joy, a voice from behind the stone called back, 'O King, live for ever. My God has sent His angel to stop the lions' mouths, and I am not hurt.' Darius quickly had the stone taken away, and Daniel was brought safely out. Then Darius wrote out a notice or proclamation saying that Daniel's God was the only true God, the only one who was really powerful, and that he wanted everyone to know it.

After this no one tried to hurt Daniel again, and he lived in the palace till he died as a very old man. In the last years of his life he had many strange dreams. They were about all that was going to happen in the world in the years to come, how there would be many kings and kingdoms, and how Someone would come into the world who would save the people and show them how to live.

The Return from the Exile

THE people of Judah had lived in Babylon for seventy years. Men and women who had come there when they were children could hardly remember their former life, while those who had been born there had never known their own city of Jerusalem. Many settled down, with houses and farms of their own, and were quite happy.

There were others, though, who never forgot that they were not in the place where God really meant them to be. Among all the Babylonian gods, they had never stopped listening to the real God. They remembered all the stories of how He had brought their great-great-great-many-great-grandfathers out of Egypt with Moses, and they told their children how He had looked after them in the wilderness and brought them to the Promised Land.

These people longed to go back, especially as news came from travellers who had been in Jerusalem that their city, which used to be so beautiful, was falling down. The Temple which Solomon had built was in ruins, and so were the walls round the city.

Now that Babylon had been taken by the Medes and Persians, Cyrus, who was a wise ruler, decided to let some of the Jews return to rebuild Jerusalem.

He gave permission to a man called Zerubbabel to go back there from Babylon, with Jeshua the High Priest, and a party of faithful men and women, to start building.

Cyrus gave back many of the gold and silver ornaments which had been taken from the Temple when Jerusalem was captured. Zerubbabel and his friends were full of hope, but when they reached Jerusalem they ran into many difficulties. The people who were living in the land did not want the Jews back unless they were going to fit in with their ways, so they tried to stop the building.

The Babylonian governor would not help either, and after a while the builders became discouraged.

At this moment two prophets called Haggai and Zechariah rose up and told them what God was saying.

Haggai said, 'God says "I am with you",' and he urged them to take heart.

'Yet now be strong, Zerubbabel,' he said, 'be strong Jeshua, son of Josedek the High Priest, and be strong all the people of the land, and work.'

Haggai told them not to be discouraged by having very little money, because God said, 'All the silver is mine and the gold is mine.' Where He led, He would provide. So the people took heart again and went on building.

Zechariah had many visions of what Jerusalem was meant to be. One of them was about the Special Person whom God was going to send. Writing of this, Zechariah said, 'Rejoice greatly, O daughter of Jerusalem. Behold thy King cometh unto thee. He is just and brings salvation. He is lowly, and comes riding on a colt, the foal of an ass.'

This was five hundred years before the Special Person came, and He did ride into Jerusalem on the foal of an ass.

Not long after Haggai and Zechariah had spoken a man called Ezra joined them from Babylon with fresh strength and help for them all, and the work went ahead.

Ezra was a priest who knew all the laws that Moses had given to his people, and one of the things he did was to get the Jews together and remind them of God's Plan for them.

He made them rebuild their faith as well as the Temple and walls of the city.

The captivity had lasted seventy years as Jeremiah had foretold, and now the people were coming back to their land again.

Nehemiah

NEHEMIAH was another of the Jews who had not forgotten about God's Plan. He was cup-bearer to a later Persian king called Artaxerxes, in Susa, the capital of Persia, a long way from Jerusalem. He always came and stood by the king at meals, and gave him what he wanted to drink. This particular king was very fond of Nehemiah, and trusted him just as the earlier kings had trusted Daniel.

One day Nehemiah had news from people whom he knew in Jerusalem that they were unhappy. The walls of the city were all broken down, many of the gates had been burnt, and everything was falling into ruins again.

This made Nehemiah extremely sad. He realised that it was all their own fault that these things had happened. But he also knew how much God cared for them, and that if they would all turn back to Him God would show them the way to pick up the Plan once more.

However, he was still feeling heavy-hearted when he went to take the king his wine. The king noticed it, and asked him what was the matter.

Nehemiah explained.

'What is it that you want me to do?' asked the king.

This was almost more than Nehemiah had hoped would happen. He asked God to help him to say the right thing, and then he answered, 'I should like you to let me go back to Jerusalem and start building it up again.'

The king asked how long it would take, and Nehemiah told him.

Then the king gave him letters to the men in charge of Jerusalem and the country round about, telling them to help him, and with some of his friends Nehemiah set out for Jerusalem.

When he arrived, he called together the few Jews who were living there, and explained that he had come to rebuild the walls of the city. They were very pleased, and said they would help.

But there were some people who were not so pleased. These were the men from the other nations who were living in Jerusalem.

They had not looked after the place or kept it at all well, but they were angry at the idea of Nehemiah and his friends building it up again and possibly taking it away from them. The leaders of this group were called Tobiah and Sanballat, and they decided to make things difficult.

Nehemiah divided his builders into teams, who took on different parts of the wall. There were the gates round the wall: the Valley gate, the Water gate, the Horse gate, the Sheep gate, which had all been burnt down. So had the walls and towers in between. Soon the work was going quite fast.

When Tobiah and Sanballat saw how well the building was going, they were not only angry, but anxious. It looked as if they might soon be turned out.

First they tried laughing at the builders, knowing that sometimes it is possible to stop people doing the right thing by making fun of them.

They would stand round the Jews, saying how silly they looked trying to build up a whole wall when there were so few of them. 'Anyway,' said Tobiah and Sanballat, 'they are building it so badly that even a fox climbing up the wall would knock it down.'

But Nehemiah knew that God had told him to build the wall, and he paid no attention.

So Tobiah and Sanballat got their friends together and made plans to stop the Jews, not only by words, but by fighting. But God showed

Nehemiah what to do. He set men on guard all round the walls to protect the builders. Some of them became discouraged, but Nehemiah arranged for all the workmen to have a sword or a spear handy all the time they were working, so that if Sanballat and Tobiah attacked they could be driven off.

Nehemiah also had a man standing on the wall by him with a trumpet which he would blow at the place where any attack came. Then everyone was to run and help.

When Sanballat and Tobiah saw how determined the Jews were, they knew that they could not win by attacking the builders. So they thought of a different way to stop them. They tried to get Nehemiah to go to a meeting to talk things over, meaning to kill him when he got there, but Nehemiah, when he listened to God, knew what they were plotting, and he did not go.

After this, Tobiah and Sanballat gave up, and in the end, in spite of all the difficulties, the wall was finished. Then Nehemiah called all the people of Israel together and reminded them again about God's Plan for them. He told them once more the story of how they came out of Egypt, and how and why things had gone wrong. He got them all to say that they were sorry, and that they would like to make a new start in the city they had rebuilt. They wrote out a promise that they would live in a better way, and several of them signed it.

Malachi

NEHEMIAH had a helper named Malachi, or 'My Messenger'. That is the meaning of Malachi in Hebrew. Malachi is the last prophet quoted in the Old Testament and the last words of all in his book are wonderful ones about the Day of the Lord.

It will be a dreadful day for people who do not listen, he wrote, but for those who do, a prophet like Elijah will come who will turn the hearts of the fathers to the children and the hearts of the children to the fathers.

'Behold, I will send My messenger, and he shall prepare My way before Me, and the Lord whom ye seek shall suddenly come to his Temple, even the messenger promised in the Covenant.'

The Children of Israel are Scattered

THOUGH the Jews had gone back to their land they did not become a free nation for nearly two thousand years. Even after Jerusalem was built up, they were attacked and ruled over by the Syrians on one side and by the Egyptians on the other. They tried to have their own kingdom and fought bravely for it; but this was a smaller idea than God had for them. He wanted them to be known not so much for their country as for their close touch with Him. The point was not what they had, but what they could give. They were being prepared for the coming of the Person who was to be the heart of God's Plan for the world. This Person was to be born into the Jewish family, though He was far greater than the Jewish people.

Because they were persecuted and invaded, many Jews were scattered to cities and countries all over the world which was known to them at that time. They made little groups of people in all these places, and took with them their belief in God who was their Father.

You remember that Hezekiah had made an end of all the sacrifices that the Jews had made to pretence gods on the hills all round the country and in Jerusalem. From that day onwards there was only one place where sacrifices could be made, and that was Jerusalem itself. So all the Jews who were scattered everywhere about the world had to do without sacrifices.

They made a rule that in any place where there were ten Jews, they could come together once a week and pray to God and listen to Him together. They could meet anywhere, in a room, in a house, or in a hall, wherever was convenient, according to how many there were. They called these gatherings 'Synagogues'. Synagogue is a Greek word which means 'Get together'. They gave the same name to the special building where they met in towns where they were a large number.

They had nothing to look at in these Synagogues, like the altar and the sacrifices in the Temple at Jerusalem. This helped them to understand even more clearly that though God is not seen, He is always there, and able to talk to anyone at any time.

They never again tried to make a god whom they could see. Some stayed on in what had been the Southern Kingdom of Judea. Others were scattered to the East and the West. All they had were the rolls on which the prophets had written what God had told them, so somebody would read from one of these rolls each week.

In this way they kept together in spirit through the strength of their idea of one God. And here for the present we will leave the story of the Jewish people.

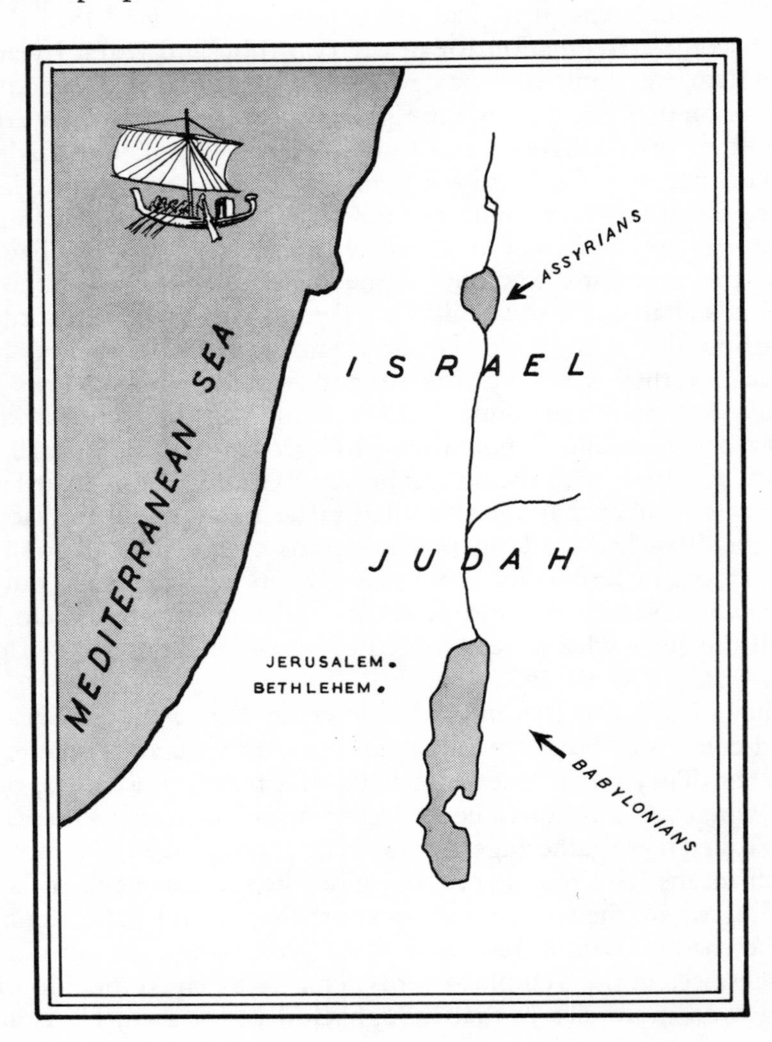

Great Men in Other Lands

THE Israelites had for more than a thousand years been fighting against the idea of gods made of stone and wood. In spite of the times when they had gone astray and tried these other gods, they always came back to God Himself. They passed on the stories about Him to their children, and took these stories with them when they were taken prisoner or had to escape to other lands.

Through trade, and even war and captivity, other countries were brought into touch with Israel's ideas about God and His Plan and His Laws. The story of these people in all their dealings with God is far the most complete one that we have of God's Plan working out through families and through a nation.

They were a people whom God specially chose, and it was into their nation that Jesus, God's Son, was born. Just as the knowledge of Jesus Christ was later to go to the whole world far beyond the Jewish people, so men of other races and countries were touched by God's Spirit.

About the time when the Jews went back to Jerusalem, thoughtful men in other lands were beginning to turn away from the gods which they saw all around them. They were reaching out for something new.

Soon there began to arise in these other countries men with great moral, or right ideas about how to live, and they were able to give these ideas to the people of their countries.

Before going on to the greatest story of all, the story of Jesus, we will look at some of these great men, and see how they fitted into God's complete pattern.

The first is Zoroaster who lived just before the Jews went back to Jerusalem.

Zoroaster

NEAR to the land of the people of Israel was the land of the Medes and Persians. Media and Persia were two different countries, which later became one when Cyrus, King of Persia, conquered Media and ruled over them both. Wherever he went, he took the law of the Medes and Persians 'which altereth not'. By their law, once an order had been given, it could never be altered. It was because of this that Darius had to throw Daniel into the lions' den.

There lived in Media, shortly before Cyrus joined it to Persia, a man named Zoroaster. He was kind-hearted and loved people and animals. When he was quite a young man, he went to help someone who was looking after the poor, but after a while he felt that just giving people food was not enough. They needed something in their hearts too. So he went away to a cave to listen to God and find out what He wanted him to do with his life.

Zoroaster believed that God could put His thoughts into men's minds; and after a while God did speak very clearly to him.

He told him to go out to the people, who felt worried and helpless, and show them a new way to live. He told Zoroaster that there would be difficulties, but that He would help him.

Up to that time Zoroaster had not been very good at talking to people or explaining things to them; but God gave him the gift of putting things clearly so that all men everywhere would understand it.

Then Zoroaster went back to his own town.

When he got there, his friends and relations were amazed to see how different he had become, and they asked him what had happened.

He said, 'God has chosen me as a prophet to give you some better ideas than the ones you have now.'

The people in Media at that time, as in many other countries, were beginning to grow out of the old beliefs about sacrificing animals, and trying not to make bad spirits angry, but they did not know what to believe instead.

Zoroaster told them that what God wanted was people who were ready to say that they were sorry for what they had done wrong, and to ask forgiveness from Him.

The important things in life were 'to have good thoughts, speak good words and do good deeds'. This was Zoroaster's favourite saying. But even though this was absolutely right, and everyone could see how different he was, few wanted to do it themselves.

The priests, who were paid much money by those who came to sacrifice in the Temple, said that he was putting people against their old ways, and they tried to get the rulers of the land to drive him out. Others tried to twist what he said to make it seem to mean something different. Some laughed at him, and others decided to kill him. Zoroaster called them the children of Evil Thoughts, and when he found that no one would listen to him, he decided to go to other countries in the east of Persia.

He went on foot, and often found that his enemies had got there before him, and had turned people against him. In time his feet became sore and his clothes wore out. He hardly ever had a chance to sleep in a bed, and he became quite discouraged.

He prayed sadly to God and said, 'In ten years only one man has listened to me.' But God encouraged him, and told him to go on.

God told him to go to the chief city of a country called Bactria, and see the king. So on Zoroaster went. He made his way to the palace and found the king. At first the priests and those who called themselves 'wise men' tried to stop him, but at the end of two years the king, Vishtaspa, was beginning to live in the same way as Zoroaster.

Things now began to go better for him. He settled in the city and married. His wife and her family took up his way of life, and so did many of their relations. The idea spread to the king of the next country, who had been an enemy of King Vishtaspa. As a result this king and Vishtaspa became friends.

From this city, Zoroaster's ways of thinking and living spread quite fast. He believed that men were meant to fight the battle between the Good Voice and the Bad Voice; that God was completely good and loving, but that there was a Bad Spirit at work too, whom he called The Lie.

Zoroaster taught that one day good would win, and that everyone could help in the fight by choosing to live in honesty and purity. The Good Spirit, said Zoroaster, could help to show people the truth, but the Bad Spirit should not be listened to.

He, or some of his later followers, believed that God was going to send someone to the earth who would be stronger than the Bad Spirit. But in the meantime people should work hard, look after the land, care for their animals, speak the truth, keep their promises, be good to the poor and look after people who were in need, especially their own families.

After he died, the Persian king, Cyrus, conquered India, where Zoroaster had lived, and joined it to Persia. Though Zoroaster was dead, his ideas were very much alive, and Cyrus was interested in them. It is thought that he put many of them into practice. At any rate, the countries over which he ruled were the best governed of any we know of in the world at that time. You will remember from the story of the Exile that it was Cyrus who conquered Babylon too. And it was Cyrus who allowed the Jews to go back to Judah and Jerusalem and build it up again. He encouraged the Jewish prince Zerubbabel to take back with him everyone who was prepared to go.

All the kings of the Medes and Persians who followed Cyrus kept up their belief in Zoroaster. So all his ideas lived on and helped to bring unity to many of the great nations of the old world.

People who follow his teaching are called Parsees.

The Buddha

FARTHER to the east of Zoroaster's country lies the great land of India. The people who lived there believed in as many different gods as did the Assyrians and Babylonians who conquered the Israelites. India was divided into many kingdoms, with rich and powerful kings. One of these kings had a son, Siddhatha Gautama. The king loved Gautama very much, and wanted him to be happy and not to know about all the unhappiness in the world. He tried to keep his son inside the palace grounds, where everything was beautiful and nobody was poor.

However, Gautama did not want to be kept in the grounds of the palace all his life, and one day he told his servant Shanna to take him for a drive outside in his chariot. The first person they saw when they got beyond the gate was a very poor old man. Gautama had never seen anybody poor before, so he asked his servant about it. Shanna replied that there were many bad things in the world about which the prince knew nothing.

This made Gautama think, and next day he asked to go out again in the chariot. Shanna drove him through the gates, and lying by the road they saw a poor man who was very ill. The prince asked about this too, and heard that many sick people in his father's kingdom had no one to care for them. He thought hard as he drove home.

On the third day he went out again, and this time they met some people carrying a dead man to be buried. No one had ever spoken to Gautama about death or dying, but when he asked Shanna about it, the servant said it was something that happened to everyone, even to princes, and that it was another of the many things Gautama had not been allowed to know about.

By now the young prince had begun to realise that although he had all he needed, and everything was done to make him happy, there were many people in his own country who had nothing, and who were poor and unhappy. He began to feel that all his riches and possessions were doing nothing to help such people, and perhaps too it was a mistake to think that people could only be happy if they were rich and comfortable.

He wished that he could do something about it. The next day when he went out, the first person he saw was a monk or holy man, standing by the side of the road. Shanna explained that this was a man who had nothing of his own, but who believed in goodness, and tried to show people how to live good lives. As he spoke, Gautama began to wonder if this was not what he should be doing. Perhaps he too could have a part in answering all the unhappiness in the world.

He went home and thought a lot more, and one night he decided that he must go right away from the palace and all his possessions, and decide what he was going to give his life to. So in the middle of the night he got up and went away, taking only his faithful Shanna with him. After walking for some days, he sat down under a tree called a Bo tree to think, and he stayed there thinking for six years.

At the end of that time a lot of things were sorted out in his mind. During those years he had seen that the way to make the world a better place was for people to have peace in their hearts. He saw that owning many things did not of itself make men happy. It very often only made them greedy. He decided to give up all his own possessions, and to give his life for the peace of the world. It was not an easy thing to decide, but he felt that if he had nothing of his own it would be easier to teach other people not to depend on the things they had.

He visited many wise men; but though he learnt much from them he was still not satisfied. He felt that there was something more which he was meant to see. Five students of one of the wise men left their leader and went to live with Gautama. At first they all thought that the way to serve God was to eat almost nothing and never allow yourself to have anything you liked. Gautama tried this for a while, but he made himself so ill that he nearly died, and he decided that it was not the right way.

Even though Gautama had been so ill, the other five men still thought that they ought to go on trying to eat nothing, and when Gautama did not agree with them, they became angry and left him.

Gautama was left quite alone, and might well have died if some girls from a village near by had not brought him food and drink and helped him to get better.

Then he began to realise that eating was not wrong. It was only wrong to eat too much. He fought against selfishness in his own heart, and also against fear, which he said was the cause of all the trouble in the world. He saw that being honest and loving was more important than being rich.

At first he wished he could find this way of living by himself and for himself, and just live it quietly without bothering other people, or being bothered by them.

But one day two men driving carts were passing by the tree where he sat, and the carts became stuck in the mud. They asked Gautama

to come and help them. As they worked to get the carts out of the mud, he talked to them about his new ideas on how to live. To his surprise, he found that they were very interested, and he began to feel that perhaps he had a message for the world.

He first tried to find the two old wise men who had been his teachers, but they had died. So he went to look for the five other men who had left him because they did not agree with him.

After searching for some time, he found them. They were still angry with him but as he came near to them and they saw how different he looked, all the anger in their hearts melted away. They said that they were sorry for their bad feelings and, after talking far into the night, they decided to join Gautama in travelling round to take his message to other people. In time many others joined them, including his cousin Ananda, who stayed with him all through his life.

He began to be known as the Buddha, which means the Enlightened One, or one who understands many things.

The Buddha Takes his Teachings to New Places

SOME people fought against the Buddha's ideas, among them one of his cousins called Devadatta, who tried to make trouble. But by this time many men in the Government were on the Buddha's side, so it came to nothing.

Once Devadatta let loose a savage elephant on him, hoping that it would kill him. The Buddha had been told this would happen, but he had no fear. He loved animals, and as the elephant reached him it became calm and knelt at his feet.

One of the ministers of the king gave some land with a house and a beautiful garden to be used by the Buddha as a school. Some merchants or business men in another part of the country clubbed together to buy him a place where he could teach people.

In time many of his own family, whom he had not seen for many years, came and joined him.

The Buddha treated everyone alike, no matter whether they were rich or poor, good or bad. One woman, who had lived a bad life, decided to give up her bad way of living, and he asked her to dinner. It surprised some of the royal personages to hear that she had been asked and not they. She, too, gave her house and garden for the Buddha to use as a school.

Though many people gave up their homes, others were not called to do so. But his teaching was the same for everyone. He told all who came asking him questions that they must be loving, honest and pure. They were not to kill or steal, nor to be lazy. They were to look after their families, obey their teachers, and care for everyone, servants and slaves as well as friends.

When one of his disciples was ill, and the others wanted to leave him somewhere, the Buddha said to them:

'Brothers, you have no father or mother to take care of you. If you do not take care of each other, who else, I ask, will do so? Brothers, if anyone wants to look after me, let him look after those who are ill.'

When he was a very old man of eighty, he was still travelling round teaching people, but he knew that the time had come for him to die.

So he called his cousin Ananda, who had been with him for many years, and said to him and others that they must not mourn, and that they should not say, 'The word of the master is ended. We have no teacher now.' 'No,' he said, 'the teaching I have given you will be your teacher when I have gone.'

He encouraged Ananda, and said he knew that he would win over all his difficulties.

'For a long time, Ananda,' he said, 'you have been very near to me by acts of love. You have done well.'

All the time he was dying, he was thinking about others. He sent for all the neighbours, and they were introduced to him family by family. Though it was late at night, men were coming all the time asking to join in his work, and he talked to them and told them how to change and live differently. He went on talking to people and encouraging them right up to the time he died. He said of himself that he was one of those who point the way.

When he died, his ideas lived on in the men he had taught, who were called Buddhists. Some were trained to be monks and to teach. If you go to countries like Burma and Ceylon you will see men dressed in yellow robes, with their heads shaved, and with calm, gentle faces. These are Buddhist priests. It was one of them who told me some of the things which I have just told you.

If you see a statue of Buddha, you will always see him looking very quiet and peaceful. But that peace had come out of a six years' struggle to know the truth. And the truth he saw was written down with the rest of the story by the Buddhist monk I have spoken of.

It was:

'Avoid all evil.
Do all good.
Purify the mind (that means, think right thoughts).
These are the words of the Lord Buddha.'

The Emperor Asoka

TWO hundred years after Buddha died, all the little kingdoms that he had known became one great kingdom or empire. The third ruler or emperor of this great empire was called Asoka.

He was used to fighting and conquering other nations and taking people prisoner and killing them. But one day he met a Buddhist monk, who told him that there was a different way of living. This made Asoka think.

He had been fighting against some neighbouring people called the Kalingas, and had done a great many cruel things. Suddenly he saw how much unhappiness he was causing to all the families whose fathers and sons he had taken prisoner, or killed. He decided to change completely, and to spend the rest of his life so that his country and the countries round about should know of Buddha's teachings.

One way in which we know about this is very interesting. King Asoka sent men to those other countries to say how sorry he was to have been so cruel to them, and he had this message carved on great rocks so that everyone could read it. It can still be read today.

Among those to whom he sent messages were the Kalingas, against whom he had been fighting when he first met the Buddhist monk.

He sent teachers far and wide to let men know what the Buddha had said. They reached many of the countries near India, and two hundred years later these ideas reached China too.

The Emperor Asoka was a great man because, though he was a powerful ruler and could have done anything he wanted to, he had the courage to start entirely new ways of running his country, beginning with himself. This led to a new spirit spreading over India which brought peace and unity for many years.

China

JUST about the time that the Buddha was sitting under the Bo tree trying to understand what was the right way to live, new ideas were beginning to take root and grow in China. This is the next big country to the east beyond India.

There were actually many different countries in China, all ruled over by an emperor. The emperor was called the Son of Heaven, and besides ruling the people, he was a priest. He had to be at services in the temples and make sacrifices, because it was believed that this made God look after the people properly.

The Chinese people used the same word for God and Heaven. They believed that there was one Great God in Heaven, but they also believed that He could show Himself to men, often in different shapes. Sometimes they thought He appeared as a dragon, and many old Chinese pictures have wonderful dragons in them with lovely curly tails.

People also felt that looking at the emperor was one way of seeing God, and in early times they all obeyed him as God. As long as the emperors were good and honourable men, this worked well, but after a while they became lazy and proud, and the people stopped respecting them.

They began to think less of the emperors and more of themselves. They stopped obeying them, even though the emperors still lived in their own palaces with courtiers round them.

In this way the people stopped keeping the rules which it was the emperor's business to see were carried out.

One of these rules was that, if there was a war, it should be fought in a polite and thoughtful way. Each side was supposed to give the other a fair chance of attacking properly. For instance, one army was never allowed to attack another while it was crossing a river. It was supposed to wait until the enemy army had got across and formed up into a line of battle.

If one army won a victory and the other escaped back into its own country, the winners were not supposed to chase them more than a few miles after they had got back to their own land. Nor was anyone allowed to cross the land of any other ruler without his permission.

When the people of China stopped obeying these rules, the different countries in China began to fight savagely against each other.

Everything became very confused, and people began to think deeply about what was the cause of all the trouble. They wondered how peace and order could be brought back to the world. At this point, many wise men, or sages, appeared, who taught others what they thought the answers were. These sages often wandered around from country to country, talking to anyone who would listen, and giving advice to any ruler who would take it.

Confucius

THE most famous sage of China was called Confucius. His Chinese name was Kung Fu-tse, but we will go on calling him Confucius in this story because that is what people in Europe have made of the name Kung Fu-tse. The Chinese always put their family name first, so his family name was Kung. The Kung family is still a famous Chinese family today.

Confucius came from quite a poor family, but he had such good ideas that many people listened to him. After a while he started a school to which most of the chief people in his country sent their sons. They were the children who were to become the future governors and rulers of China.

Confucius taught people not so much about God as about good ideas. Like the Buddha and Zoroaster, he taught men how to live right and think for other people.

He taught that people should obey all the old rules of politeness and courtesy, and that children should respect their parents. But the most important thing he taught was that everyone should have something that the Chinese called 'jen', something like caring or love. We might call it great-heartedness.

If you did not have great-heartedness you were not worth much, Confucius thought. If someone tried to make you do something that was wrong, it was better even, he said, to be killed than to stop being great-hearted towards others.

In time Confucius became the king's adviser. He arranged for poor people to be given food, had good roads made, built bridges and stopped strong men being cruel to weak ones. He said the princes and head men in the country must not become too powerful, because a few men ordering all the others about never makes a happy country.

The king, whose adviser Confucius was, liked these ideas, but the neighbouring king, a very powerful man, did not like them. He felt that they might break his power. So he thought that he would persuade Confucius' king to think about something different.

He sent Confucius' king a lot of presents. He sent dancers to amuse him, and conjurers, and monkeys, and many interesting things. And I am sorry to say that the result was just what he had hoped.

The man who had been a good king gradually became more and more interested in the dancers and the conjurers, and less and less interested in what Confucius was trying to say to him.

Confucius was deeply disappointed. He waited for a while, hoping that the king would turn to him again and ask for his help, but he never did. So Confucius went away to live in another country.

He lived there for many years till the king died, and the next king asked him to come back.

Unfortunately, by that time Confucius was too old to do much to help the king. However, he spent the remaining years of his life writing down all the things in which he believed. These books were kept and handed down, and can still be read today.

When he died, he thought that all his work and thinking had been wasted. But he was wrong. For many thousands of years his ideas were the ones by which people lived in China.

Mo-Tsu

ONE of the followers of Confucius was Mo-Tsu. In spite of all that Confucius had done, wars went on getting fiercer. Mo-Tsu said that Confucius' teaching did not go far enough. Mo taught absolute love and unselfishness. He said, 'Take God as your standard. God wants men to love, and does not want them to hate and hurt each other. Obey the will of God. That is the standard of doing right.'

Confucius had taught that you ought to have more love for some people, your parents, for example, than for others. But Mo said that you ought to love everyone the same. All the wrong things in the world, all the wars and troubles, were due to hatred, he said, and there was only one answer to this, and that was love.

People said that it would not work, and other sages called him mad. He said that his madness was better than quarrelling or bickering. That really was a kind of madness, and the only way to stop someone being nasty to you was to love him and care for him. He said that this was the way to stop wars.

'The way of absolute love is to think of the countries of others as your own, and the families of others as your own. Now, when everyone thinks of the countries of others as he does of his own, who would attack those countries? When everyone thinks of the houses of others as his own, who would seize those houses?

'It is the will of God to love everyone everywhere,' he said. 'When lords and rulers love one another, there will be no more war. When heads of houses love one another, there will be no more seizing of each other's houses and lands.'

The only place to begin, he said, was with yourself. If you wanted somebody else to love your parents, then you must love their parents first.

All men were equal in the sight of Mo. The children of poor men came to his school as well as the children of rich and powerful men. All were treated alike, and many of them became statesmen later on.

He himself lived on simple food and wore workman's clothes. Even those who did not agree with his ideas could not help respecting him. He wore himself out doing good, for not only did he teach in his school, but he travelled constantly from place to place wherever there was trouble, trying to bring an answer.

'On entering a country, one should see where the need is, and work on that,' he said.

Once when he heard that one large state was threatening a small one, he walked ten days and ten nights to try and help. His feet became so sore that he had to tear pieces off his clothes to wrap them up.

However, even when he succeeded in stopping attacks, people were not always grateful; but he seldom felt discouraged or complained.

In spite of some people being against him, he had many followers, and groups of them met together regularly in the towns and cities in order to plan how to bring the new spirit to the nation.

Unfortunately, the people as a whole did not listen to Mo's message. In one country in particular, the ruler and his advisers followed quite a different idea, namely, that you must force people to be obedient and become united. These rulers built up a powerful army, and conquered all the remaining free countries of China one after the other. The conqueror called himself 'The First August Emperor'. Everyone had to obey his orders. He laid down what people should believe, and gave orders that all the books containing any other ideas should be burnt. In this way the books which contained Mo's teaching were almost entirely destroyed.

This emperor did not last long, and the next one tried to bring back the ideas of Mo-Tsu and Confucius. Eventually his empire came to an end too, amidst terrible wars and sufferings for the ordinary people. It was then that the followers of Mo-Tsu joined up with some of the followers of the Buddha who had found their way from India to China: there were Chinese Buddhists and a few Indian teachers, and now, while people were hungry for an answer, they had a good opportunity to spread their ideas. Together they gave the people new hope and new standards.

So the Chinese people recovered, and their country became united again. It brought in the greatest age of China, in which for a while the ideas and teaching of Buddha, Confucius and Mo-Tsu all played a part.

Greece

COMING back from India and China to the part of the world where we started, you will find the land of Greece. It is a beautiful wild country, made up partly of steep mountains and partly of islands that lie around the coast.

Greece is a small land in the blue, sunny Mediterranean Sea; but it has left great gifts to the world.

Not long after David was building Jerusalem and singing his psalms, a great Greek poet, Homer, was telling the story of the wars and adventures of the Greek heroes in poetry which people have since read and loved through the centuries.

When Jeremiah was warning the Jews of their danger and pointing the way for them to the only true God, Greek wise men were beginning to study nature, discovering the way it worked and writing about it so cleverly that people followed what they said for hundreds of years.

And when the Jews were returning from Babylon to build Jerusalem again, Greek poets and historians were writing plays and histories which everyone ever since has admired as some of the greatest in the world.

Greek philosophers, or 'lovers of wisdom', at the same time wrote down truths about human nature, and the way they saw men are meant to live, on their own and together. And Greek sculptors made statues, some of which still remain in honoured places in our galleries and museums.

Greek builders built temples and famous buildings, often using the shining marble stone which is found around the Mediterranean lands. You can still see and wonder at the remains of these buildings in Athens and other places.

In the fifth century before Christ came, the Greeks had built up what were called City States. Each city with the countryside around it was like a little nation, each with its own laws and government. Because these city states were small compared with the size of an ordinary country, each citizen came to feel responsible for the whole city.

Everyone was allowed to say what he thought should be done, everyone, that is to say, except the slaves, of whom there were a good many. But full responsibility, even for free men, was a new idea. The Greek cities were among the first groups of people to try what we call Democracy, which means 'Government by the people', from two Greek words meaning 'people' and 'rule'. The people decide who is to rule them. Every grown-up person has a part. And when the rulers whom they have chosen propose their laws and plans, the people have to approve or disapprove before anything is done. It is from this idea that the governments of many nations of today have grown, and it works so long as everybody really does feel responsible.

The Persian kings, who began to let some of the Jews go back to Jerusalem from Babylon, also tried to capture Greece. But all the Greek cities banded together in face of this danger, and in several battles on land and sea they drove the invading armies back and saved their homes. The stories of the courage of the Greek soldiers in these battles has become a legend which has been told and retold for nearly two thousand five hundred years.

Soon, however, the Greek cities fought among themselves, because though there were many wise and clever men in Greece, they had no great idea which they all accepted, no idea strong enough and good enough to make them really united.

Socrates

SOCRATES was one of the great thinkers of ancient Greece, whose ideas, had they been followed in his own age, might have made a great difference to Greek history.

Socrates believed that it was very important always to find out what was really right.

The Greeks believed in a whole family of gods and goddesses, of whom the Father was called Zeus, and the Mother, Hera. They imagined that these two had many children, who married sea nymphs and wood spirits and many other creatures. They told their children wonderful stories about the adventures of these gods and goddesses. The stories have been handed down and put in books.

Socrates believed in some of the Greek gods himself. But he also believed in an extra something, which the people around him did not. From the time he was quite small he had heard a voice speaking in his heart, telling him what he should and should not do. He had come to obey this voice, which he believed was a special friendly spirit who belonged to him and who was sent specially to look after him. It often stopped him from doing wrong or unwise things.

It is thought that he started life as a sculptor. Many people earned their living by making statues of the various gods and goddesses, and also of famous leaders, as there were no cameras in those days to take photographs.

Athens, the city which was Socrates' home, joined at this time in a war against another Greek state. Socrates was a soldier, like all the Athenians. But in the middle of the battle of Potidaea he began to think of the tragedy of a world where men killed each other and destroyed good things. He stood stock-still for twenty-four hours while the battle raged all round him. In this long and strange time of quiet, the Voice showed him that he should spend the rest of his life showing men how to change their ways of living and thinking.

After this, Socrates liked talking to people better than making statues of them. He longed to help them to think straight and understand what things were true.

To understand other people, he tried very hard to understand himself. He wanted to find the truth and to help other people to find it.

He happily spent whole days sitting and talking to people in the streets of Athens, in the market-place and in his home. He once said he did not really like going out into the country because there were no people there, and he felt that much the most important thing in the world was to talk to people and help them.

You would have thought that the rulers in Athens would have been glad to have in their city someone like Socrates. But they were not.

For Socrates taught people to ask questions about everything. He taught them first to question themselves. He made them wonder if they were doing right or not, and that led on to their questioning many other things, such as the way the city was run, things that nobody had ever questioned before. It made the rulers angry, and they said Socrates was teaching young men to be disrespectful to their elders.

They did not like Socrates' 'small voice'. They said there were plenty of perfectly good gods without having another who might not only upset the people, but might overthrow all the old gods as well.

What was happening in their minds, though they did not recognise it, was what happens nearly every time somebody with a new idea comes along. The men who are running things naturally like their own way of doing things. When someone comes along who thinks rather differently, the men in power can either say to themselves, 'Let's see if this man is right and try out his ideas', or they can say, 'If this man turns out to be right, perhaps I shall turn out to be wrong. Let's get rid of him.'

And this was what the rulers of Athens felt about Socrates. He was a man with much bigger ideas than theirs, and they could not understand what he was talking about.

So they arrested him and brought him to be judged, partly, they said, for making young people disrespectful, partly for trying to upset the old gods. But Socrates stood firmly by all he felt to be true.

He said that he had not tried to turn men from the old gods. He said that he believed in them all still, though he also believed that there was one Great God who really did make everything and was above the others. He said that he had not turned people against their rulers, but he did believe in helping men to think for themselves, and decide what is right.

Socrates and his judges argued for a long time. There were some who agreed with him, but most of them did not. In the end, the men who were against him won, and were allowed to say what his punishment should be.

One said that he should be killed. But according to the law of the country it was only a suggestion, and Socrates was asked if he had any other punishment to suggest.

'Punishment!' said Socrates. 'Of course not. You do not punish people for being right. You only punish them for being wrong. Think of all I have done for this city. You ought to give me a house to live in and look after me for the rest of my life.'

This made the judges extremely angry. They had thought that he would suggest going to prison for a while, or paying some money as a fine. They were so angry that after a while Socrates' friends managed to persuade him to offer to pay a fine.

But the judges had had enough of Socrates. They felt that if he were dead he would not give them any more bother, and they said he must die by drinking poison.

But Socrates had no fear of death. He said that dying was only a door which led to finding something more about what was really true. He said he would sooner die than say that his teaching was wrong. He was put in prison, and all his friends came to see him till finally the day came for him to drink the poison. Then he quietly drank it and died. All through the time of waiting he talked to his friends and helped them to think straight.

He was a brave man who had the courage to stick to what he knew deep in his heart was right, no matter what other people said, or what happened to him.

His teachings, and those of other wise men who knew him or were taught by him, are still used today to help people think things out for themselves.

Alexander the Great

THERE are two kinds of people in the world: those who like to tell others what to do, and those who like to be ordered about and grumble because of it.

People more easily fall into these two groups when they stop obeying God. The Israelites and the Jews, when they stopped following God, always looked for someone or something else to follow. It was either a golden calf, or a king, or being clever, or strong, or rich. Then they would begin to think more of themselves than of God; and at this point some other nation always attacked and defeated them.

After the time of Socrates the people who lived round the Mediterranean Sea felt very confused. The old gods had lost a lot of their power over men's minds. The Jewish people were scattered, or ruled by foreign kings. People were divided and quarrelling with each other, when about 356 B.C., there appeared a man who had an idea.

His name was Alexander, and the idea was that he would conquer all the countries of the world he knew and rule over them. You may not think this was a good idea, but it was a big one and Alexander believed in it.

As no one had a bigger or a better plan, he started to carry it out. He raised armies, and really made his soldiers want to conquer the world. In a very few years he had swept across Persia right into India, and back again to Egypt, defeating everyone who stood in his path.

I have put him in because men like Alexander keep cropping up in history when people lose their faith, that is to say, when they stop following God's Plan for them.

All the same, there was more in Alexander than just the idea of conquering other countries, and because of it he is called Alexander the Great. Somewhere he had inside him the idea of making the whole world live in peace after he had conquered it.

Actually this does not work, as you all know from your own families, at the times when your parents say 'Stop quarrelling or you will be punished.' Alexander, however, really wanted something more than punishment for people. He tried to turn the world he knew into one family by making his generals and soldiers marry ladies belonging to the conquered countries.

He held an enormous wedding at which hundreds of couples were married at the same time. He also called people to a great service at which he prayed to whatever God there was, that all men might now be brothers and live in peace.

It did not work, though. It takes more than a big wedding and services to stop people being selfish and wanting their own way, and when Alexander died soon afterwards, these same generals started quarrelling about who should rule the different parts of his empire. The Persian and Indian parts soon broke up, but Alexander left his mark all around the eastern end of the Mediterranean.

The city of Alexandria in Egypt, which is still a busy port today, was called after him. The language he spoke, which was Greek, went on being used in those parts for several hundred years. It became a language through which ideas could pass from one country to another, and through which men from different countries were able to know and understand each other.

Towards the New Age

ALL this time men's minds and hearts were reaching out for something new.

The ideas of Buddha, Confucius and Zoroaster were spreading round the places where they had lived. The ideas of Socrates and other wise men from Greece were taking root too. The Jews themselves had taken the news of what they knew of God to Assyria and Babylon when they were in exile there, and also to the lands round the Mediterranean Sea.

In some countries people still believed in different gods and goddesses, or thought that gods were made of wood or stone, or lived in seas and forests. But they were beginning to feel that the time of the old gods was coming to an end.

The world was waiting for something new.

What was it going to be?

The Jews had been told by God that He was going to send a Special Person into the world to save it and bring something wholly new to men. Many prophets and wise men had spoken and written of His coming.

The next book will tell how He came.

Thine ears shall hear a word behind thee, saying, This is the way, walk ye in it.

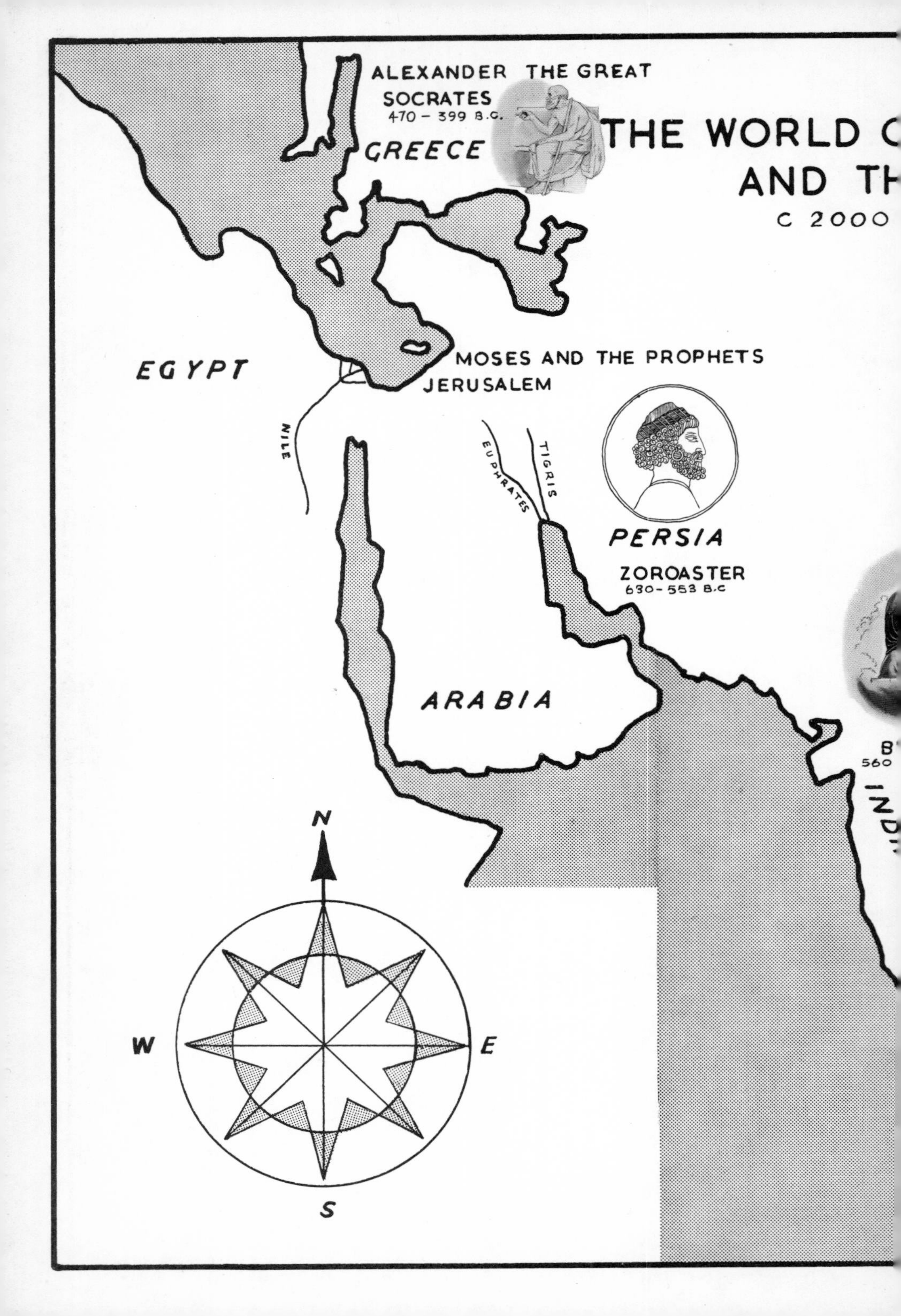

ALEXANDER THE GREAT
SOCRATES
470 – 399 B.C.
GREECE
THE WORLD C
AND TH
C 2000
EGYPT
MOSES AND THE PROPHETS
JERUSALEM
NILE
EUPHRATES
TIGRIS
PERSIA
ZOROASTER
630 – 553 B.C
ARABIA
560
N
W
E
S